Funeral Services
of the Christian
Churches in England

Fourth Edition

Including additional hymn section

CANTERBURY PRESS NORWICH

Canterbury Press Norwich
13A Hellesdon Park Road, Norwich NR6 5DR

Canterbury Press Norwich is a publishing imprint of
Hymns Ancient and Modern Limited, a registered charity

Standard print: ISBN 978 1 85311 984 2
Large print: ISBN 978 1 84825 106 9

Second Impression 1987
Further Impressions 1988, 1990
Fifth Impression 1992, including new Roman Catholic Funeral Rite
Sixth Impression 1993
First New Edition 1994, including additional hymn section
Further Impressions 1995, 1997, 1999
Second New Edition 2001, with new services and extra hymns
Further Impressions 2001, 2002, 2003, 2005
Fourth Edition 2009
Second Impression 2011
Third Impression 2012

Typeset by David Lewis XML Associates, Bungay
Printed in the UK by MPG Books Ltd, Bodmin, Cornwall

CONTENTS

CHURCHES REPRESENTED ON THE CHURCHES' FUNERALS GROUP

The Baptist Union of Great Britain
The Church in Wales
The Church of England
The Methodist Church
The Oriental Orthodox Churches
The Orthodox Churches
The Roman Catholic Church
The Salvation Army
The United Reformed Church

in consultation with
The Free Churches Group and
The Free Church Council of Wales

PREFACE

In the compilation of this book the primary aim has been to make it as helpful as possible to those who are suffering under the burden and stress of grief. If this has been achieved it will also assist those who are responsible for the ordering of funeral services at cemeteries and crematoria.

Many who are faced with the loss of someone they have loved may not be able to bring to their situation the hope and strength of a well-tested and familiar Christian faith. It is our hope that, for them, these services may afford perhaps not only comfort and support but also an opportunity for reflection and fresh spiritual understanding.

Whilst first and foremost the preparation of the book has been an exercise in co-operation between the Christian churches, it has at the same time involved consultation with a number of organisations which share responsibility with the Churches for the arrangement of funeral services. The Churches' Funerals Group (the Churches' representative body on whose initiative the book has been published) wishes to record its warm appreciation of the wisdom, skill and dedication of all who in any capacity have taken part in this work. Among them, special gratitude is due to the publishers, the Canterbury Press Norwich.

It is our prayer that all who use the services in this book may know the healing love of God in their time of loss and sorrow.

✠ GEOFFREY GIBRALTAR

The Funeral Service for use at a cemetery or crematorium

prepared by the Joint Liturgical Group

THE SHAPE OF THE RITE

Gathering
Welcome and Introduction
Tribute
Ministry of the Word
Prayers
Commendation
Lord's Prayer
Committal
Prayers for our continuing journey towards heaven
Blessing

THE GATHERING

The coffin may be received by the minister.

One or more sentences of scripture may be used.

'I am the resurrection and the life,' says the Lord. 'Those who believe in me, even though they die, will live, and everyone who lives and believes in me will never die' *John 11.25,26*

Blessed are those who mourn, for they will be comforted. *Matthew 5.4*

God so loved the world that he gave his only Son, so that everyone who believes in him may not perish but may have eternal life. *John 3.16*

Come to me all who labour and are heavy laden and I will give you rest. *Matthew 11.28*

The steadfast love of the Lord never ceases, his mercies never come to an end; they are new every morning. *Lamentations 3.22,23*

In the world you have tribulation; but be of good cheer, I have overcome the world. *John 16.33*

God is our refuge and strength, a very present help in trouble. *Psalm 46.1*

Blessed be the God and Father of our Lord Jesus Christ! By his great mercy God has given us a new birth into a living hope through the resurrection of Jesus Christ from the dead, and into an inheritance that is imperishable, undefiled and unfading. *I Peter 1: 3-4b*

WELCOME AND INTRODUCTION

The minister uses these or similar words.

We meet in this solemn moment to worship God;
to give thanks for the life of our *sister/brother N;*
to commend *her/him* to God's loving and faithful care;
and through our love and prayers
to comfort each other in our grief.

In the presence of death,
Christ offers us sure ground
for hope, confidence and joy,
because he has shared our human life and death,
has been raised triumphant from the dead
and lives for evermore.

In Christ we have eternal life
and through him
God our Father welcomes us into the glory of heaven.
Methodist Worship Book, 1999 (adapted)

A hymn may be sung.

TRIBUTE

Words of appreciation for the person who has died may be
given here, or woven into the sermon or said by the minister
before or during the prayer of thanksgiving.

OPENING PRAYER

Let us pray:

A short silence

Either

God our comforter,
you are our refuge and strength,
a helper close at hand in times of trouble.
Help us so to hear your word
that our fears may be dispelled,
our loneliness eased,
and our hope in you reawakened.
May your Holy Spirit lift us above our sorrow,
into the light and peace of your constant love;
and this we ask through Jesus Christ our Lord. **Amen.**
A New Zealand Prayer Book, 1989

or

Loving God, you brought us to birth,
and at our last hour you welcome us into your presence.
As we rejoice in the promise of resurrection
may the darkness of death be turned
into the dawn of new life,
and the sorrow of parting
into the of joy of heaven;
through our Saviour Jesus Christ,
who died, and rose again
and lives for evermore. **Amen.**
A New Zealand Prayer Book, 1989 (adapted)

THE MINISTRY OF THE WORD

Let us hear the words of Holy Scripture.

One or more of the following or other Bible readings and psalms are used.

READINGS FROM THE OLD TESTAMENT

For everything there is a time

For everything its season,
and for every activity under heaven its time:
a time to be born and a time to die;
a time to plant and a time to uproot;
a time to kill and a time to heal;
a time to break down and a time to build up;
a time to weep and a time to laugh;
a time for mourning and a time for dancing;
a time to scatter stones and a time to gather them;
a time to embrace and a time to abstain from embracing;
a time to seek and a time to lose;
a time to keep and a time to discard;
a time to tear and a time to mend;
a time for silence and a time for speech;
a time to love and a time to hate;
a time for war and a time for peace.

God has made everything to suit its time;
and has given to all a sense of past and future,
but no comprehension of his work from beginning to end.
I know that whatever God does lasts for ever;
there is no adding to it, no taking away.
And God has done it in such a way
that everyone must feel awe in his presence.
Ecclesiastes 3:1-8, 11, 14

They shall mount up with wings

Have you not known? Have you not heard?
The Lord is the everlasting God,
the Creator of the ends of the earth.
He does not grow faint or weary;
his understanding is unsearchable.
He gives power to the faint,
and strengthens the powerless.
Even youths will faint and be weary,
and the young will fall exhausted;
but those who wait for the Lord will renew their strength,
they shall mount up with wings like eagles,
they shall run and not be weary,
they shall walk and not faint. *Isaiah 40.28-31*

A READING FROM THE APOCRYPHA

They are in peace

The souls of the righteous are in the hand of God,
and no torment will ever touch them.
In the eyes of the foolish they seemed to have died,
and their departure was thought to be a disaster,
and their going from us to be their destruction;
but they are in peace.
For though in the sight of others they were punished,
their hope is full of immortality.
Having been disciplined a little,
they will receive great good,
because God tested them
and found them worthy of himself. *Wisdom 3.1-5, 9*

THE PSALMS

The Lord is my shepherd

The Lord is my shepherd, I shall not want.
He makes me lie down in green pastures;
he leads me beside still waters;
he restores my soul.
He leads me in paths of righteousness for his name's sake.
Even though I walk through the valley of the shadow of death,
I fear no evil;
for you are with me;
your rod and your staff – they comfort me.
You prepare a table before me in the presence of my enemies;
you anoint my head with oil;
my cup overflows.
Surely goodness and mercy shall follow me
all the days of my life,
and I shall dwell in the house of the Lord
my whole life long. *Psalm 23*

Also these psalms:

Psalm 27
Psalm 90
Psalm 103
Psalm 121

READINGS FROM THE NEW TESTAMENT

In my Father's house

Jesus said to his disciples:
'Do not let your hearts be troubled.
You believe in God, believe also in me.
In my Father's house there are many dwelling-places.
If it were not so,
would I have told you that I go to prepare a place for you?
And if I go to prepare a place for you,
I will come again and will take you to myself,
so that where I am, there you may be also.
And you know the way to the place where I am going.
Thomas said to him,
'Lord we do not know where you are going.
How can we know the way?
Jesus said to him, 'I am the way, and the truth, and the life.
No one comes to the Father except through me.' *John 14.1-6*

The resurrection of Christ

Very early on the first day of the week, when the sun had risen, Mary Magdalene, and Mary the mother of James, and Salome went to the tomb. They had been saying to one another, 'Who will roll away the stone for us from the entrance to the tomb?' When they looked up, they saw that the stone, which was very large, had already been rolled back. As they entered the tomb, they saw a young man, dressed in a white robe, sitting on the right side, and they were alarmed. But he said to them, 'Do not be alarmed; you are looking for Jesus of Nazareth, who was crucified. He has been raised; he is not here. Look, there is the place they laid him. *Mark 16.2-6*

Nothing can separate us from God's love

What then are we to say about these things? If God is for us,
who is against us? He who did not withhold his own Son, but
gave him up for us all, will he not with him also give us
everything else? Who will bring any charge against God's elect?
It is God who justifies. Who is to condemn? It is Christ Jesus,
who died, yes, who was raised, who is at the right hand of God,
who intercedes for us.
Who will separate us from the love of Christ? Will hardship, or
distress, or persecution, or famine, or nakedness, or peril, or
sword? As it is written,
> For your sake we are being killed all day long;
> We are counted as sheep to be slaughtered.'
No, in all these things we are more than conquerors through
him who loved us. For I am convinced that neither death, nor
life, nor angels, nor rulers, nor things present, nor things to
come, nor powers, nor height, nor depth, nor anything in all
creation, will be able to separate us from the love of God in
Christ Jesus our Lord. *Romans 8.31-38*

All are made alive in Christ

Christ has been raised from the dead, the first fruits of those
who have died. For since death came through a human being,
the resurrection of the dead has also come through a human
being; for as all die in Adam, so all will be made alive in Christ.

When this perishable puts on imperishability, and this mortal
puts on immortality, then the saying that is written will be
fulfilled:
> 'Death has been swallowed up in victory.'
> 'Where, O death, is your victory?'
> 'Where, O death, is your sting?'

9

The sting of death is sin, and the power of sin is the law. But thanks be to God, who gives us the victory through our Lord Jesus Christ. *1 Corinthians 15.20-22, 53-57*

The holy city, the new Jerusalem

I saw a new heaven and a new earth;
for the first heaven and the first earth had passed away,
and the sea was no more.
And I saw the holy city, the new Jerusalem,
coming down out of heaven
as a bride adorned for her husband.
And I heard a loud voice from the throne saying,

'See, the home of God is among mortals.
He will dwell with them;
they will be his peoples,
and God himself will be with them;
he will wipe every tear from their eyes.
Death will be no more;
mourning and crying and pain will be no more,
for the first things have passed away.'

And the one who was seated on the throne said,
'See, I am making all things new.'
Then he said to me,
'Write this, for these words are trustworthy and true.'
Then he said to me, 'It is done!
I am the Alpha and the Omega, the beginning and the end.
To the thirsty I will give water
as a gift from the spring of the water of life.
Those who conquer will inherit these things,
and I will be their God and they will be my children.'
Revelation 21.1-7

A sermon is preached.

A hymn may be sung.

THE PRAYERS

PRAYERS OF THANKSGIVING

One of the following may be used.

Either

Let us give thanks for the victory of Christ over death and let us recall the life we have shared with N.

Silence

Father of all,
we give you thanks and praise for the goodness and love
revealed in your creation.
In your great love for the world
you gave your only Son, our Saviour Jesus Christ,
to be the companion of our journey
and the sharer of our sorrows;
By his cross and passion
Christ has conquered the power of death
and by his resurrection
he has opened for us all the way to eternal life.

We bless you for the great company of faithful men and women
whom Christ has brought through death,
who now behold your face in glory
and for whose light and example we now give you praise.

Today we give you thanks for N and for our memories of *her/him*.

We praise you for your steadfast love
which followed *her/him* through all the days of *her/his* life,
and for love and gifts which *she/he* shared with us.

We thank you for all than *N* has meant to us,
and that for *her/him*death is now past.
We pray that you will bring us all
into your eternal kingdom
where together with *N* we shall enjoy your presence for ever.
Amen.

or (after a short life or a stillbirth)

As we remember the days and hours that *N* was part of our life:
let us give thanks for the victory of Christ over death.

Silence

Loving Father,
we give you thanks that we are made
in your image and likeness
and that in your Son our Saviour Jesus Christ
you have overcome the sharpness of death.

We remember in your presence, *N*
whose hold on earthly life has ended,
and we pray that you will continue to work in *her/him*
the good purpose of your perfect will;
through the same Christ our Lord. **Amen.**

PRAYERS FOR THOSE WHO MOURN

Let us remember *N's* family and friends,
(especially we pray for . . . .)

One of the following prayers may be used.

God of compassion,
we pray for those who mourn today
and for those whose need of you is very great.
May they embrace your promise of eternal life
and, in their grief,
receive your gifts of peace, hope, joy and faith;
through Christ our Lord. **Amen.**
Worship from the United Reformed Church, 2003 (adapted)

Almighty God,
Father of all mercies and giver of all comfort,
deal graciously with those who mourn,
that, casting every care on you
they may know the consolation of your love;
through Jesus Christ our Lord. **Amen.**
Bishop Slattery, English and American Prayer Books, 1928

Eternal God,
you are the Lord of life, the Conqueror of death,
our help in every time of trouble
and you do not willingly grieve or afflict your children.
Comfort those who mourn
and give us grace in the presence of death
to worship you,
that we may have sure hope of eternal life
and be enabled to put our whole trust
in your goodness and mercy;
through Jesus Christ our Lord. **Amen.**
W. E. Orchard, Divine Service, 1919

Father of mercies and God of all comfort,
you love all that you have made
and you have created nothing in vain.
Comfort us in our sorrow,
surround us with your presence
and console us with the knowledge of your unfailing love;
through Jesus Christ our Lord. **Amen.**
Baptist Gathering for Worship, 2005 (altered)

Grant us, O God,
in all our duties your help,
in all our perplexities your guidance,
in all our dangers your protection,
and in all our sorrows your peace;
through Jesus Christ our Lord. **Amen.**

O God from whom we flee,
whose stillness is more terrible
than earthquake, wind, or fire,
speak to our loneliness
and challenge our despair;
that in your very absence
we may recognize your voice,
and wrapped in your presence
we may go forth to encounter the world,
in the name of Christ. **Amen.**
*Janet Morley, All Desires Known, 1988 (based on
1 Kings 19.9-18)*

Gracious God,
surround us today with your compassion.
Do not let grief overwhelm us,
nor anguish of heart turn us from you.

14

In our darkness
let the light of your love still shine within us
and in our pain and loss
let the peace of your presence continue to fill our lives;
through Christ our Lord. **Amen.**

At the death of a child

God of compassion,
we bless you for the joy that Jesus found
in the company of children,
and for his assurance
that the kingdom of heaven belongs to them.
In the hour of this our deepest sorrow
help us to know your love.
In our perplexity help us to trust in you.
In our loneliness grant us your peace
and in our pain the strength of your presence;
through Christ our Lord. **Amen.**

After a sudden or violent death

Lord,
you have promised that you will not abandon us
in the hour of despair.
Help us to remember
that your light outshines all darkness,
your love covers all sin
and your risen presence brings peace at the last;
and this we ask for your own name's sake. **Amen**
Baptist Gathering for Worship, 2005 (altered)

A hymn may be sung.

THE COMMENDATION

The minister stands by the coffin and may invite others to gather around it.

The minister says

Let us commend *N* to God.

Either

Into your keeping, O merciful God,
we commend your servant *N*
Receive *her/him* into the arms of your mercy,
into the joy of everlasting peace,
and into the glorious company of the saints in light;
through Christ our Lord. **Amen.**
Methodist Worship Book, 1999

or

Loving God,
We commend *N* to your perfect mercy and wisdom, for in you alone we put our trust. **Amen.** *Methodist Worship Book, 1999*

THE LORD'S PRAYER

Either

As our Saviour taught his disciples, we pray:

**Our Father who art in heaven,
hallowed be thy Name,
thy kingdom come,
thy will be done,
on earth as it is in heaven.
Give us this day our daily bread.
And forgive us our trespasses
as we forgive those who trespass against us.**

And lead us not into temptation;
but deliver us from evil.
For thine is the kingdom,
the power and the glory,
for ever and ever. Amen.

or

We say together the prayer that Jesus gave us:

Our Father in heaven,
hallowed be your Name;
your kingdom come,
your will be done
on earth as in heaven.
Give us today our daily bread,
Forgive us our sins,
as we forgive those who sin against us.
Save us from the time of trial
and deliver us from evil.
For the kingdom,
the power and the glory are yours,
now and for ever. Amen.

When the whole service takes place in a crematorium or
cemetery chapel or at the graveside, the service continues with
the Committal.

If there is a procession from the cemetery chapel to the graveside the minister says

God grant to the living, grace;
to the departed, rest;
to the world, peace;
and to us and all the faithful, life everlasting;
and the blessing of God,
the Father, the Son and the Holy Spirit,
be with *you/us* now and for ever. **Amen.**

The minister, going before the body to the grave, may say one or more of these sentences.

As a Father pities his children, so the Lord pities those who fear him. For he knows our frame; he remembers that we are dust. *Psalm 103.13*

Blessed be the God and Father of our Lord Jesus Christ, the Father of mercies and God of all comfort, who comforts us in all our affliction. *2 Corinthians 1.3*

To this end Christ died and lived again, that he might be Lord both of the dead and of the living. *Romans 14.9*

THE COMMITTAL

The minister says

either

The earthly life of *N* has come to an end,
we therefore commit *her/his* body
to be cremated/to be buried,
earth to earth, ashes to ashes, dust to dust;
in sure and certain hope
of the resurrection to eternal life
through our Lord Jesus Christ;
to whom be the glory for ever and ever. **Amen.**
Methodist Worship Book, 1999 (altered)

or

God alone is holy and just and good.
in this certainty we have commended *N* to God.
We therefore commit *her/his* body
to be cremated/to be buried,
earth to earth, ashes to ashes, dust to dust;
trusting in the infinite mercy of God,
through Jesus Christ our Lord. **Amen.**
Methodist Worship Book, 1999 (altered)

PRAYERS FOR OUR CONTINUING JOURNEY TOWARDS HEAVEN

One or more of the following may be used.

Support us, O Lord, all the day long,
until the shadows lengthen, and the evening comes,
the busy world is hushed,
the fever of life is over and our work is done.
Then, in your mercy, grant us a safe lodging,
a holy rest, and peace at the last;
through Jesus Christ our Lord. **Amen.**
John Henry Newman, Sermon on Wisdom and Innocence, 1829
(adapted)

Heavenly Father,
in your Son Jesus Christ,
you have given us a true faith, and a sure hope:
help us to live as those who believe and trust
in the communion of saints,
the forgiveness of sins,
and the resurrection to life everlasting,
and strengthen this faith and hope in us
all the days of our life:
through the love of your Son our Saviour. **Amen.**
Prayer Book as proposed in 1928

Bring us, O Lord our God,
at our last awakening,
into the house and gate of heaven,
to enter into that gate,
and dwell in that house,
where there shall be
no darkness nor dazzling,
but one equal light;

no noise nor silence,
but one equal music;
no fears nor hopes,
but one equal possession;
no ends nor beginnings,
but one equal eternity;
in the habitation of your glory and dominion,
world without end. **Amen.**
*Eric Milner-White, based on a sermon preached by John Donne
in 1628*

Father of all,
by whose mercy and grace
your saints remain in everlasting light and peace:
we remember with thanksgiving
those whom we love but see no longer;
and we pray that in them
your perfect will may be fulfilled;
through Jesus Christ our Lord. **Amen.**
Prayer Book as proposed in 1928 (adapted)

Eternal Lord God, you hold all souls in life:
shed forth, we pray,
upon your whole Church in paradise and on earth
the bright beams of your light and heavenly comfort;
and grant that we,
following the good example of those who have loved
and served you here and are now at rest,
may at the last enter with them
into the fullness of your eternal joy;
through Jesus Christ our Lord. **Amen.**
William Temple, 1881-1944

A hymn may be sung.

21

THE BLESSING

One of the following may be used.

The peace of God
which passes all understanding,
keep *your/our* hearts and minds
in the knowledge and love of God
and of his Son, Jesus Christ our Lord;
and the blessing of God,
the Father, the Son and the Holy Spirit,
remain with *you/us* always. **Amen.**

or

May God in his infinite love and mercy
bring the whole Church,
living and departed in the Lord Jesus,
to a joyful resurrection
and the fulfilment of his eternal kingdom;
and the blessing of God,
the Father, the Son and the Holy Spirit,
remain with *you/us* always. **Amen.**

or

The God of peace,
who brought again from the dead our Lord Jesus,
that great shepherd of the sheep,
make you perfect in every good work to do his will,
and the blessing of God,
the Father, the Son and the Holy Spirit,
remain with *you/us* always. **Amen.**

The Funeral Service

from COMMON WORSHIP
Services and Prayers for
the Church of England

PASTORAL INTRODUCTION

This may be read by those present before the service begins.

God's love and power extend over all creation. Every life, including our own, is precious to God. Christians have always believed that there is hope in death as in life, and that there is new life in Christ after death.

Even those who share such faith find that there is a real sense of loss at the death of a loved one. We will each have had our own experiences of their life and death, with different memories and different feelings of love, grief and respect. To acknowledge this at the beginning of the service should help us to use this occasion to express our faith and our feelings as we say farewell as well as acknowledge our loss and our sorrow, and reflect on our own mortality. Those who mourn need support and consolation. Our presence here today is part of that continuing support.

The Funeral Service

STRUCTURE

THE GATHERING

[Sentences]
Introduction
[Prayer]
[Prayers of Penitence]
The Collect

READINGS AND SERMON

PRAYERS

COMMENDATION AND FAREWELL

THE COMMITTAL

THE DISMISSAL

The Funeral Service

THE GATHERING

The coffin may be received by the minister
One or more sentences of scripture may be used.

'I am the resurrection and the life,' says the Lord. 'Those who believe in me, even though they die, will live, and everyone who lives and believes in me will never die.' *John 11.25, 26*

I am convinced that neither death, nor life, nor angels, nor rulers, nor powers, nor things present, nor things to come, nor height, nor depth, nor anything else in all creation, will be able to separate us from the love of God in Christ Jesus our Lord. *Romans 8.38, 39*

Since we believe that Jesus died and rose again, even so, through Jesus, God will bring with him those who have died. So we will be with the Lord for ever. Therefore encourage one another with these words. *1 Thessalonians 4.14, 17, 18*

We brought nothing into the world, and we take nothing out. The Lord gave, and the Lord has taken away; blessed be the name of the Lord. *1 Timothy 6.7; Job 1.21*

The steadfast love of the Lord never ceases, his mercies never come to an end; they are new every morning; great is his faithfulness. *Lamentations 3.22–23*

Blessed are those who mourn, for they will be comforted. *Matthew 5.4*

God so loved the world that he gave his only Son, so that everyone who believes in him may not perish but may have eternal life. *John 3.16*

INTRODUCTION

The minister says

We meet in the name of Jesus Christ,
who died and was raised to the glory of God the Father.
Grace and mercy be with you.

The minister introduces the service in these or other suitable
words

We have come here today
to remember before God our *brother/sister N*;
to give thanks for *his/her* life;
to commend *him/her* to God our merciful redeemer and judge;
to commit *his/her* body to be *buried/cremated*,
and to comfort one another in our grief.

The minister may say this prayer

God of all consolation,
your Son Jesus Christ was moved to tears
at the grave of Lazarus his friend.
Look with compassion on your children in their loss;
give to troubled hearts the light of hope,
and strengthen in us the gift of faith,
in Jesus Christ our Lord. **Amen.**

A hymn may be sung. With the minister's agreement, suitable
symbols of the life and faith of the departed person may be
placed on or near the coffin, and a brief tribute may be spoken
by the minister, a family member or friend.

PRAYERS OF PENITENCE

These words may be used

As children of a loving heavenly Father,
let us ask his forgiveness,
for he is gentle and full of compassion.

God of mercy
we acknowledge that we are all sinners.
We turn from the wrong that we have thought and said
     and done,
and are mindful of all that we have failed to do.
For the sake of Jesus, who died for us,
forgive us for all that is past,
and help us to live each day
in the light of Christ our Lord. **Amen.**

(or)

Lord, have mercy.
Lord, have mercy.
Christ, have mercy.
Christ, have mercy.
Lord, have mercy.
Lord, have mercy.

The minister may say

May God our Father forgive us our sins,
and bring us to the eternal joy of his kingdom
where dust and ashes have no dominion. **Amen.**

THE COLLECT

Merciful Father,
hear our prayers and comfort us;
renew our trust in your Son,
whom you raised from the dead;
strengthen our faith
that all who have died in the love of Christ
will share in his resurrection;
who lives and reigns with you,
in the unity of the Holy Spirit
one God now and for ever. **Amen.**

READINGS AND SERMON

A reading from the Old or New Testament may be read.
The psalm may be in a metrical or hymn version, or be
replaced by a scriptural song.

PSALM 23

1 The Lord is my shepherd;
    therefore can I lack nothing.

2 He makes me lie down in green pastures
    and leads me beside still waters.

3 He shall refresh my soul
    and guide me in the paths of righteousness for his name's
    sake.

4 Though I walk through the valley of the shadow of death,
       I will fear no evil;
    for you are with me;
       your rod and your staff, they comfort me.

29

5 You spread a table before me
    in the presence of those who trouble me;
you have anointed my head with oil
    and my cup shall be full.

6 Surely goodness and loving mercy shall follow me
    all the days of my life,
and I will dwell in the house of the Lord for ever.

or

PSALM 90

1 Lord, you have been our refuge
    from one generation to another.

2 Before the mountains were brought forth,
    or the earth and the world were formed,
from everlasting to everlasting you are God.

3 You turn us back to dust and say:
'Turn back, O children of earth.'

4 For a thousand years in your sight are but as yesterday,
which passes like a watch in the night.

5 You sweep them away like a dream;
they fade away suddenly like the grass.

6 In the morning it is green and flourishes;
in the evening it is dried up and withered.

7 For we consume away in your displeasure;
we are afraid at your wrathful indignation.

8 You have set our misdeeds before you
and our secret sins in the light of your countenance.

9 When you are angry, all our days are gone;
our years come to an end like a sigh.

10 The days of our life are three score years and ten,
     or if our strength endures, even four score;
  yet the sum of them is but labour and sorrow,
     for they soon pass away and we are gone.

11 Who regards the power of your wrath
  and your indignation like those who fear you?

12 So teach us to number our days
  that we may apply our hearts to wisdom.

13 Turn again, O Lord; how long will you delay?
  Have compassion on your servants.

14 Satisfy us with your loving-kindness in the morning,
  that we may rejoice and be glad all our days.

15 Give us gladness for the days you have afflicted us,
  and for the years in which we have seen adversity.

16 Show your servants your works,
  and let your glory be over their children.

17 May the gracious favour of the Lord our God be upon us;
  prosper our handiwork; O prosper the work of our hands.

A reading from the New Testament (which may be a Gospel Reading) is used.

A sermon is preached.

PRAYERS

A minister leads the prayers of the people.
The prayers usually follow this sequence:
— Thanksgiving for the life of the departed
— Prayer for those who mourn
— Prayers of penitence (if not already used)
— Prayer for readiness to live in the light of eternity

This form may be used.

God of mercy, Lord of life,
you have made us in your image
to reflect your truth and light:
we give you thanks for *N*,
for the grace and mercy *he/she* received from you,
for all that was good in *his/her* life,
for the memories we treasure today. (Especially ...)

You promised eternal life to those who believe.
Remember for good this your servant *N*
as we also remember *him/her*.
Bring all who rest in Christ
into the fullness of your kingdom
where sins have been forgiven
and death is no more.

Your mighty power brings joy out of grief
and life out of death.
Look in mercy on (... *and*) all who mourn.
Give them patient faith in times of darkness.
Strengthen them with the knowledge of your love.

You are tender towards your children
and your mercy is over all your works.
Heal the memories of hurt and failure.
Give us the wisdom and grace to use aright
the time that is left to us here on earth,
to turn to Christ and follow in his steps
in the way that leads to everlasting life.

God of mercy,
entrusting into your hands all that you have made
and rejoicing in our communion
    with all your faithful people,
we make our prayers
    through Jesus Christ our Saviour. **Amen.**

The Lord's Prayer may be said.

As our Saviour taught us, so we pray

**Our Father in heaven,
hallowed be your name,
your kingdom come,
your will be done,
on earth as in heaven.
Give us today our daily bread.
Forgive us our sins
as we forgive those who sin against us.
Lead us not into temptation
but deliver us from evil.
For the kingdom, the power,
and the glory are yours
now and for ever. Amen.**

(or)

Let us pray with confidence as our Saviour has taught us:

**Our Father, who art in heaven,
hallowed be thy name;
thy kingdom come;
thy will be done;
on earth as it is in heaven.
Give us this day our daily bread.
And forgive us our trespasses,
As we forgive those who trespass against us.
And lead us not into temptation;
but deliver us from evil.
For thine is the kingdom,
the power and the glory,
for ever and ever. Amen.**

COMMENDATION AND FAREWELL

The minister stands by the coffin and may invite others to gather around it.

The minister says

Let us commend *N* to the mercy of God
our maker and redeemer.

Silence is kept.

The minister uses this or another prayer of entrusting and commending.

God our creator and redeemer,
by your power Christ conquered death
and entered into glory.
Confident of his victory
and claiming his promises,
we entrust *N* to your mercy
in the name of Jesus our Lord,
who died and is alive
and reigns with you,
now and for ever. **Amen.**

THE COMMITTAL

Sentences of scripture may be used.

The Minister says

either

The Lord is full of compassion and mercy:
slow to anger and of great goodness.
As a father is tender towards his children:
so is the Lord tender to those that fear him.
For he knows of what we are made:
he remembers that we are but dust.
Our days are like the grass;
we flourish like a flower of the field;
when the wind goes over it, it is gone:
and its place will know it no more.
But the merciful goodness of the Lord
    endures for ever and ever
    toward those that fear him:
and his righteousness upon their children's children.

(or)

We have but a short time to live.
Like a flower we blossom and then wither;
like a shadow we flee and never stay.
In the midst of life we are in death;
to whom can we turn for help,
but to you, Lord, who are justly angered by our sins?

Yet, Lord God most holy, Lord most mighty,
O holy and most merciful Saviour,
deliver us from the bitter pain of eternal death.
Lord, you know the secrets of our hearts;
hear our prayer, O God most mighty;
spare us, most worthy judge eternal;
at our last hour let us not fall from you,
O holy and merciful Saviour.

The minister uses one of the following forms of Committal.

At the burial of a body

We have entrusted our *brother/sister* N to God's mercy
and we now commit *his/her* body to the ground:
earth to earth, ashes to ashes, dust to dust:
in sure and certain hope of the resurrection to eternal life
through our Lord Jesus Christ,
who will transform our frail bodies
that they may be conformed to his glorious body,
who died, was buried, and rose again for us.
To him be glory for ever. **Amen.**

(or)

in a crematorium, if the Committal is to follow at the Burial of
the Ashes

We have entrusted our *brother/sister* N to God's mercy,
and now, in preparation for burial,
we give *his/her* body to be cremated.
We look for the fullness of the resurrection
when Christ shall gather all his saints
to reign with him in glory for ever. **Amen.**

(or)

in a crematorium, if the Committal is to take place then

We have entrusted our *brother/sister N* to God's mercy,
and we now commit *his/her* body to be cremated:
earth to earth, ashes to ashes, dust to dust
in sure and certain hope of the resurrection to eternal life
through our Lord Jesus Christ,
who will transform our frail bodies
that they may be conformed to his glorious body,
who died was buried, and rose again for us.
To him be glory for ever. **Amen.**

THE DISMISSAL

This may include one or more of the following

The Lord's Prayer (if not used earlier: see p. 33)

NUNC DIMITTIS (The Song of Simeon)

Lord now you let your servant go in peace:
your word has been fulfilled.

My own eyes have seen the salvation:
which you have prepared in the sight of every people;

a light to reveal you to the nations:
and the glory of your people Israel.

Glory to the Father and to the Son:
and to the Holy Spirit;
as it was in the beginning is now:
and shall be for ever. **Amen.**

One or more of these prayers, or other suitable prayers

Heavenly Father,
in your Son Jesus Christ
you have given us a true faith and a sure hope.
Strengthen this faith and hope in us all our days,
that we may live as those who believe in
   the communion of saints,
   the forgiveness of sins
   and the resurrection to eternal life;
through Jesus Christ our Lord. Amen.

God be in my head,
and in my understanding;
God be in my eyes,
and in my looking;
God be in my mouth,
and in my speaking;
God be in my heart,
and in my thinking;
God be at my end,
and at my departing. Amen.

THE BLESSING

May God give *you*
his comfort and his peace,
his light and his joy,
in this world and the next;
and the blessing of God almighty,
the Father, the Son, and the Holy Spirit,
be upon *you* and remain with *you always*. **Amen.**

READINGS

John 14.1–6

Jesus said to his disciples: 'Do not let your hearts be troubled. Believe in God, believe also in me. In my Father's house there are many dwelling places. If it were not so, would I have told you that I go to prepare a place for you? And if I go and prepare a place for you, I will come again and will take you to myself, so that where I am, there you may be also. And you know the way to the place where I am going.' Thomas said to him, 'Lord, we do not know where you are going. How can we know the way?' Jesus said to him, 'I am the way, and the truth, and the life. No one comes to the Father except through me.'

1 Corinthians 15.20–26, 35–38, 42–44A, 53–end

But in fact Christ has been raised from the dead, the first fruits of those who have died. For since death came through a human being, the resurrection of the dead has also come through a human being; for as all die in Adam, so all will be made alive in Christ. But each in his own order: Christ the first fruits, then at his coming those who belong to Christ. Then comes the end, when he hands over the kingdom to God the Father, after he has destroyed every ruler and every authority and power. For he must reign until he has put all his enemies under his feet. The last enemy to be destroyed is death.

But someone will ask, 'How are the dead raised? With what kind of body do they come?' Fool! What you sow does not come to life unless it dies. And as for what you sow, you do not sow the body that is to be, but a bare seed, perhaps of wheat or of some other grain. But God gives it a body as he has chosen, and to each kind of seed its own body.

So it is with the resurrection of the dead. What is sown is perishable, what is raised is imperishable. It is sown in dishonour, it is raised in glory. It is sown in weakness, it is raised in power. It is sown a physical body, it is raised a spiritual body.

For this perishable body must put on imperishability, and this mortal body must put on immortality. When this perishable body puts on imperishability, and this mortal body puts on immortality, then the saying that is written will be fulfilled:

'Death has been swallowed up in victory.'
'Where, O death, is your victory?
Where, O death, is your sting?'

The sting of death is sin, and the power of sin is the law. But thanks be to God, who gives us the victory through our Lord Jesus Christ.

Therefore, my beloved, be steadfast, immovable, always excelling in the work of the Lord, because you know that in the Lord your labour is not in vain.

Revelation 21.1–7

I, John, saw a new heaven and a new earth; for the first heaven and the first earth had passed away, and the sea was no more. And I saw the holy city, the new Jerusalem, coming down out of heaven from God, prepared as a bride adorned for her husband. And I heard a loud voice from the throne saying,

'See, the home of God is among mortals.
He will dwell with them;
they will be his peoples,
and God himself will be with them;
he will wipe every tear from their eyes.
Death will be no more;
mourning and crying and pain will be no more,
for the first things have passed away.'

And the one who was seated on the throne said, 'See, I am making all things new.' Also he said, 'Write this, for these words are trustworthy and true.' Then he said to me, 'It is done! I am the Alpha and the Omega, the beginning and the end. To the thirsty I will give water as a gift from the spring of the water of life. Those who conquer will inherit these things, and I will be their God and they will be my children.'

ALTERNATIVE READINGS:

John 6.35–40; John 11.17–27; Romans 8.31–38; 1 Corinthians 15.20–58; 1 Thessalonians 4.13–18

An Order for the Funeral of a Child

THE GATHERING

One or more sentences of scripture may be used. (See also
p. 26.)

I am convinced that neither death, nor life, nor angels, nor
rulers, nor powers, nor things present, nor things to come, nor
height, nor depth, nor anything else in all creation, will be able
to separate us from the love of God in Christ Jesus our Lord.
Romans 8.38, 39

The Lamb who is at the throne will be their shepherd, and will
lead them to springs of living water, and God will wipe away all
tears from their eyes. *Revelation 7.17*

Beloved, we are God's children now; what we will be has not
yet been revealed. What we do know is this: when he is
revealed, we will be like him, for we will see him as he is.
1 John 3.2

I will comfort you, says the Lord, as a mother comforts her
child, and you shall be comforted. *Isaiah 66.13*

The minister welcomes the people and introduces the service
in these or other suitable words

We have come together to worship God,
to thank him for his love,
and to remember the [short] life on earth of *N......*;
to share our grief
and to commend *him/her* to the eternal care of God.

The minister may say this prayer

O God, who brought us to birth,
and in whose arms we die,
in our grief and shock,
contain and comfort us;
embrace us with your love,
give us hope in our confusion,
and grace to let go into new life;
through Jesus Christ. **Amen.**

A tribute or tributes may be made.

Authorized Prayers of Penitence may be used.

The Collect may be said here or in the Prayers.

READINGS AND SERMON

One or more Readings from the Bible. The following may be
suitable for particular occasions.
Psalm 23; Psalm 84.1–4; The Song of Solomon 2.10–13;
Isaiah 49.15–16; Jeremiah 1.4–8; Jeremiah 31.15–17;
Matthew 18.1–5, 10; Mark 10.13–16; John 6.37–40; John
10.27, 28; Romans 8.18, 28, 35, 37–39; 1 Corinthians 13.1–
13; Ephesians 3.14–19.

Psalms or hymns may follow the readings.

A Sermon is preached.

PRAYERS

The prayers usually follow this sequence:

— Thanksgiving for the child's life, however brief
— Prayer for those who mourn
— Prayers of penitence (if not already used)
— Prayer for readiness to live in the light of eternity.

The Lord's Prayer may be said.

As our Saviour taught us, so we pray

Our Father in heaven,
hallowed be your name,
your kingdom come,
your will be done,
on earth as in heaven.
Give us today our daily bread.
Forgive us our sins
as we forgive those who sin against us.
Lead us not into temptation
but deliver us from evil.
For the kingdom, the power,
and the glory are yours
now and for ever. Amen.

(or)

Let us pray with confidence as our Saviour has taught us:

Our Father, who art in heaven,
hallowed be thy name;
thy kingdom come;
thy will be done;
on earth as it is in heaven.
Give us this day our daily bread.
And forgive us our trespasses,
As we forgive those who trespass against us.
And lead us not into temptation;
but deliver us from evil.
For thine is the kingdom,
the power and the glory,
for ever and ever. Amen.

COMMENDATION AND FAREWELL

The minister stands by the coffin and may invite others to gather around it.

The child is commended to God, with these or other authorized words.

God our creator and redeemer,
by your power Christ conquered death
and returned to you in glory
confident of your victory
and claiming his promises,
we entrust *N* to your keeping
in the name of Jesus our Lord,
who, though he died, is now alive
and reigns with you and the Holy Spirit
now and for ever. **Amen.**

(or, for a baby)

To you, gentle Father,
we humbly entrust this child so precious in your sight.
Take *him/her* into your arms
and welcome *him/her* into your presence
where there is no sorrow nor pain,
but the fullness of peace and joy with you
for ever and ever. **Amen.**

(or, for a young child)

Heavenly Father,
whose Son our Saviour
took little children into his arms and blessed them:
receive, we pray, your child *N*
in your never-failing care and love,
comfort all who have loved *him/her* on earth,
and bring us all to your everlasting kingdom;
through Jesus Christ our Lord. **Amen.**

45

(or, for an older child)

Into your hands, Lord,
our faithful creator and most loving redeemer,
we commend your child *N*,
for *he/she* is yours in death as in life.
In your great mercy
gather *him/her* into your arms
and fulfil in *him/her* the purpose of your love;
that, rejoicing in the light
    and refreshment of your presence,
he/she may enjoy that life which you have prepared
    for all those who love you,
through Jesus Christ our Lord. **Amen.**

THE COMMITTAL

The minister uses one of the following forms of Committal.

At the burial of a body

We have entrusted *N* to God's mercy,
and we now commit *his/her* body to the ground:
earth to earth, ashes to ashes, dust to dust:
in sure and certain hope of the resurrection to eternal life
through our Lord Jesus Christ,
who will transform our frail bodies
that they may be conformed to his glorious body,
who died, was buried, and rose again for us.
To him be glory for ever. **Amen.**

or

in a crematorium, if the Committal is to follow at the Burial of
the Ashes

We have entrusted *N* to God's merciful keeping,
and now, in preparation for *his/her* burial,

46

we give *his/her* body to be cremated.
We look for the fullness of the resurrection
when Christ shall gather all his saints
to reign with him in glory for ever. **Amen.**

or

in a crematorium, if the Committal is to take place then

We have entrusted *N* to God's merciful keeping,
and we now commit *his/her* body to be cremated:
earth to earth, ashes to ashes, dust to dust
in sure and certain hope of the resurrection to eternal life
through our Lord Jesus Christ,
who will transform our frail bodies
that they may be conformed to his glorious body,
who died, was buried, and rose again for us.
To him be glory for ever. **Amen.**

THE DISMISSAL

May Christ the Good Shepherd
enfold you with love,
fill you with peace,
and lead you in hope,
to the end of your days;
and the blessing of God Almighty,
the Father, the Son, and the Holy Spirit,
be among you and remain with you always. **Amen.**

(or)

May the love of God and the peace of the Lord Jesus Christ
bless and console you,
and all who have known and loved *N*,
this day and for ever more. **Amen.**

A Selection of Prayers which may be used

Gathering

God our refuge and strength,
close at hand in our distress;
meet us in our sorrow and lift our eyes
to the peace and light of your constant care.
Help us so to hear your word of grace
that our fear will be dispelled by your love,
our loneliness eased by your presence
and our hope renewed by your promises
in Jesus Christ our Lord. **Amen.**

Thanksgiving

Father in heaven, we praise your name
for all who have finished this life loving and trusting you,
for the example of their lives,
the life and grace you gave them,
and the peace in which they rest.
We praise you today for your servant *N*
and for all that you did through *him/her*.
Meet us in our sadness,
and fill our hearts with praise and thanksgiving,
for the sake of our risen Lord, Jesus Christ. **Amen.**

Those who mourn

Almighty God,
Father of all mercies and giver of all comfort:
deal graciously, we pray, with those who mourn,
that casting all their care on you,
they may know the consolation of your love;
through Jesus Christ our Lord. **Amen.**

Lord Jesus Christ,
you comforted your disciples when you were going to die:
now set our troubled hearts at rest
and banish our fears.
You are the way to the Father:
help us to follow you.
You are the truth:
bring us to know you.
You are the life:
give us that life,
to live with you now and for ever. **Amen.**

For readiness to live in the light of eternity

Support us, O Lord,
all the day long of this troublous life.
until the shadows lengthen and the evening comes,
the busy world is hushed,
the fever of life is over,
and our work is done.
Then, Lord, in your mercy
grant us a safe lodging,
a holy rest, and peace at the last;
through Christ our Lord. **Amen.**

Eternal God, our maker and redeemer,
grant us [with *N*] and all the faithful departed,
the sure benefits of your Son's saving passion
    and glorious resurrection:
that, in the last day,
when you gather up all things in Christ,
we may with them enjoy the fullness of your promises;
through Jesus Christ your Son our Lord,
who is alive and reigns with you,
in the unity of the Holy Spirit,
one God, now and for ever. **Amen.**

Grant us, Lord,
the wisdom and the grace
to use aright the time
that is left to us on earth.
Lead us to repent of our sins,
the evil we have done
and the good we have not done;
and strengthen us to follow the steps of your Son,
in the way that leads to the fullness of eternal life;
through Jesus Christ our Lord. **Amen.**

Entrusting and Commending

Heavenly Father,
you have assured us
that everyone who looks to your Son
and believes in him
shall have eternal life.
Trusting in your faithfulness,
we commend *N* to your mercy
as we await that great day
when you raise us with *him/her* to life in triumph
and we shall stand before you,
with all your whole creation made new in him,
in the glory of your heavenly kingdom. **Amen.**

Give rest, O Christ, to your servant with the saints:
where sorrow and pain are no more,
neither sighing, but life everlasting.
You only are immortal, the creator and maker of all:
and we are mortal, formed from the dust of the earth.
and unto earth shall we return.
For so you ordained when you created me, saying:
'Dust you are and to dust you shall return.'

All of us go down to the dust,
yet weeping at the grave, we make our song:
Alleluia alleluia alleluia
Give rest, O Christ, to your servant with the saints:
where sorrow and pain are no more,
neither sighing, but life everlasting.

At the funeral of a child

Lord, we pray for those who mourn,
for parents and children,
friends and neighbours.
Be gentle with them in their grief.
Show them the depths of your love,
a glimpse of the kingdom of heaven.
Spare them the torment of guilt and despair.
Be with them as they weep
   beside the empty tomb
   of our risen Saviour. **Amen.**

Father,
You know our hearts and share our sorrows.
We are hurt by our parting
   from *N* whom we loved:
when we are angry at the loss we have sustained,
when we long for words of comfort,
yet find them hard to hear,
turn our grief to more patient faith,
our affliction to firmer hope
in Jesus Christ our Lord. **Amen.**

The Burial of Ashes

If the service begins in church or chapel, it may be appropriate to invite the mourners to the place of burial at the end of the Readings, and to use Psalm 16 verses 5–11 or Psalm 139 verses 1–11, 13 at the place of burial.

PREPARATION

The minister greets the people in these or other suitable words.

Grace, mercy and peace
from God our Father and the Lord Jesus Christ
be with you all.

Though we are dust and ashes
God has prepared for those who love him
a heavenly dwelling place.
At *his/her* funeral we commended *N* into the
hands of almighty God.
As we prepare to commit the remains of *N* to the earth
we entrust ourselves and all who love God
to his loving care.

Appropriate Sentences of Scripture may be used.

The eternal God is our refuge,
and underneath are the everlasting arms. *Deuteronomy 33.27 (AV)*

Blessed be the God and Father of our Lord Jesus Christ!
By his great mercy he has given us a new birth
   into a living hope through the resurrection of Jesus
   Christ from the dead,
and into an inheritance that is imperishable, undefiled,
   and unfading,
kept in heaven for you. *1 Peter 1.3–4*

52

Lord, you have been our refuge
from one generation to another:

Before the mountains were brought forth,
  or the earth and the world were formed,
from everlasting to everlasting you are God.

You turn us back to dust and say:
'Turn back, O children of earth.'

For a thousand years in your sight are but as yesterday,
which passes like a watch in the night. *Psalm 90.1–4*

READINGS

The following may be used: Job 19.23–27
                           Psalm 16.4–10
                           Psalm 139.1–11, 13
                           1 Cor 15.35–38; 42–44a
                           John 19.38–end
                           Revelation 21–end, 22.3b–5

THE COMMITTAL

The minister says

either

We have entrusted our *brother/sister N* to God's mercy,
and we now commit *his/her* mortal remains to the ground:
earth to earth, ashes to ashes, dust to dust:
in sure and certain hope of the resurrection to eternal life
through our Lord Jesus Christ,
who will transform our frail bodies
that they may be conformed to his glorious body,
who died, was buried, and rose again for us.
To him be glory for ever. **Amen.**

or

God our Father,
in loving care your hand has created us,
and as the potter fashions the clay
you have formed us in your image.
Through the Holy Spirit
you have breathed into us the gift of life.
In the sharing of love you have enriched our knowledge
    of you and of one another.
We claim your love today,
as we return these ashes to the ground
in sure and certain hope of the resurrection to eternal life.

The congregation may join with the minister in saying

**Thanks be to God who gives us the victory
through Jesus Christ our Lord. Amen.**

PRAYERS

THE LORD'S PRAYER

**Our Father, who art in heaven,
hallowed be thy name;
thy kingdom come;
thy will be done;
on earth as it is in heaven.
Give us this day our daily bread.
And forgive us our trespasses,
As we forgive those who trespass against us.
And lead us not into temptation;
but deliver us from evil.
For thine is the kingdom,
the power and the glory,
for ever and ever. Amen.**

Heavenly Father,
we thank you for all those whom we love
   but see no longer.
As we remember *N* in this place
hold before us our beginning and our ending,
the dust from which we come
and the death to which we move,
with a firm hope in your eternal love and purposes for us,
in Jesus Christ our Lord. **Amen.**

Other prayers may be used, ending with

God of hope,
grant that we, with all who have believed in you,
may be united in the full knowledge of your love
and the unclouded vision of your glory;
through Jesus Christ our Lord. **Amen.**

THE DISMISSAL

May the infinite and glorious Trinity,
the Father, the Son and the Holy Spirit,
direct our life in good works,
and after our journey through this world
grant us eternal rest with all the saints,
in Jesus Christ our Lord. **Amen.**

The Funeral Service

Church of England
(Series One – Traditional Language)

The Service for the Funeral of a Child is not printed separately, but the appropriate paragraphs are indicated by two green asterisks** This does not exclude the use of other material.

THE INTRODUCTION

The Ministers meeting the body at the entrance and going before it shall say one or more of the following sentences.

I am the resurrection and the life, saith the Lord: he that believeth in me, though he were dead, yet shall he live; and whosoever liveth and believeth in me shall never die.
St John 11.25–26

I know that my Redeemer liveth, and that he shall stand up at the last upon the earth: whom I shall see for myself, and mine eyes shall behold, and not another. *Job 19.25–27*

We brought nothing into this world, and it is certain we can carry nothing out. The Lord gave, and the Lord hath taken away; blessed be the name of the Lord. *1 Timothy 6.7; Job 1.21*

Remember not the sins and offences of my youth: but according to thy mercy think thou upon me, O Lord, for thy goodness. *Psalm 25.6*

The eternal God is thy refuge, and underneath are the everlasting arms. *Deuteronomy 33.27*

Neither death, nor life, nor angels, nor principalities, nor powers, nor things present, nor things to come, nor height, nor depth,

nor any other creature, shall be able to separate us from the love of God, which is in Christ Jesus our Lord.
Romans 8.38–39

Whether we live, we live unto the Lord; and whether we die, we die unto the Lord: whether we live therefore, or die, we are the Lord's. For to this end Christ both died, and rose, and revived, that he might be Lord both of the dead and living.
Romans 14.8–9

Blessed are they that mourn: for they shall be comforted.
St. Matthew 5.4

Let not your heart be troubled: ye believe in God, believe also in me. In my Father's house are many mansions. *St. John 14.1*

The following is suitable at the funeral of a child.

**He shall feed his flock like a shepherd: he shall gather the lambs with his arms, and carry them in his bosom. *Isaiah 40.11*

Then shall be read one or both of these PSALMS following. At the end of all the Psalms the *Gloria Patri* may be left unsaid, and instead thereof may be sung or said

Rest eternal grant unto them, O Lord: and let light perpetual shine upon them.

Before and after any Psalm or group of Psalms may be said or sung the Anthem following.

O Saviour of the world, who by thy Cross and precious Blood hast redeemed us: Save us and help us, we humbly beseech thee, O Lord.

PSALM 90

1 Lord, thou hast been our refuge:
from one generation to another.

2 Before the mountains were brought forth,
    or ever the earth and the world were made:
thou art God from everlasting, and world without end.

3 Thou turnest man to destruction:
again thou sayest, Come again, ye children of men.

4 For a thousand years in thy sight are but as yesterday:
seeing that is past as a watch in the night.

5 As soon as thou scatterest them, they are even as a sleep:
and fade away suddenly like the grass.

6 In the morning it is green, and groweth up:
but in the evening it is cut down, dried up,
    and withered.

7 For we consume away in thy displeasure:
and are afraid at thy wrathful indignation.

8 Thou hast set our misdeeds before thee:
and our secret sins in the light of thy countenance.

9 For when thou art angry all our days are gone:
we bring our years to an end, as it were a tale
    that is told.

10 The days of our age are threescore years and ten;
    and though men be strong, that they come to
    fourscore years:
yet is their strength then but labour and sorrow;
    so soon passeth it away, and we are gone.

11 But who regardeth the power of thy wrath:
   for even thereafter as a man feareth,
     so is thy displeasure.

12 So teach us to number our days:
   that we may apply our hearts unto wisdom.

13 Turn thee again, O Lord, at the last:
   and be gracious unto thy servants.

14 O satisfy us with thy mercy, and that soon:
   so shall we rejoice and be glad all the days of our life.

15 Comfort us again now after the time that thou hast
     plagued us:
   and for the years wherein we have suffered adversity.

16 Shew thy servants thy work:
   and their children thy glory.

17 And the glorious Majesty of the Lord our God be upon us:
   prosper thou the work of our hands upon us,
     O prosper thou our handy-work.

   Glory be to the Father, and to the Son:
   and to the Holy Ghost;

   As it was in the beginning, is now, and ever shall be:
   world without end. Amen

**PSALM 23

1 The Lord is my shepherd:
   therefore can I lack nothing.

2 He shall feed me in a green pasture:
   and lead me forth beside the waters of comfort.

3 He shall convert my soul:
    and bring me forth in the paths of righteousness,
        for his name's sake.

4 Yea, though I walk through the valley of the shadow
        of death, I will fear no evil:
    for thou art with me;
        thy rod and thy staff comfort me.

5 Thou shalt prepare a table before me
        against them that trouble me:
    thou hast anointed my head with oil,
        and my cup shall be full.

6 But thy loving-kindness and mercy shall follow me
        all the days of my life:
    and I will dwell in the house of the Lord for ever.

Glory be to the Father, and to the Son:
and to the Holy Ghost;

As it was in the beginning, is now, and ever shall be:
world without end. Amen.

Then shall be read the LESSON following

1 Corinthians 15.20–26, 35–38, 42–44, 53–58

Now is Christ risen from the dead, and become the first-fruits of them that slept. For since by man came death, by man came also the resurrection of the dead. For as in Adam all die, even so in Christ shall all be made alive. But every man in his own order: Christ the first-fruits; afterward they that are Christ's, at his coming. Then cometh the end, when he shall have delivered up the kingdom to God, even the Father; when he shall have put down all rule, and all authority, and power. For he must reign, till he hath put all enemies under his feet. The last enemy that shall be destroyed is death.

But some man will say, How are the dead raised up? and with what body do they come? Thou fool, that which thou sowest is not quickened, except it die. And that which thou sowest, thou sowest not that body that shall be, but bare grain, it may chance of wheat, or of some other grain: But God giveth it a body, as it hath pleased him, and to every seed his own body. So also is the resurrection of the dead: It is sown in corruption; it is raised in incorruption: It is sown in dishonour; it is raised in glory: It is sown in weakness; it is raised in power: It is sown a natural body; it is raised a spiritual body. For this corruptible must put on incorruption, and this mortal must put on immortality. So when this corruptible shall have put on incorruption, and this mortal shall have put on immortality; then shall be brought to pass the saying that is written, Death is swallowed up in victory. O death, where is thy sting? O grave, where is thy victory? The sting of death is sin, and the strength of sin is the law. But thanks be to God, which giveth us the victory through our Lord Jesus Christ. Therefore, my beloved brethren, be ye steadfast, unmovable, always abounding in the work of the Lord, forasmuch as ye know that your labour is not in vain in the Lord.

Or at the funeral of a child

**St Mark 10.13–16

They brought young children to him, that he should touch them: and his disciples rebuked those that brought them. But when Jesus saw it, he was much displeased, and said unto them, Suffer the little children to come unto me, and forbid them not; for of such is the kingdom of God. Verily I say unto you, Whosoever shall not receive the kingdom of God as a little child, he shall not enter therein. And he took them up in his arms, put his hands upon them, and blessed them.

ALTERNATIVE READINGS 2 Cor. 4.16—5.10;
Rev. 7.4–17; Rev. 21.1–7

THE PRAYERS

Then shall the Minister say

**Let us pray.
> Lord, have mercy upon us.
> **Christ, have mercy upon us.**
> Lord, have mercy upon us.

Our Father, which art in heaven,
Hallowed be thy name;
Thy kingdom come;
Thy will be done;
In earth as it is in heaven.
Give us this day our daily bread.
And forgive us our trespasses,
As we forgive them that trespass against us.
And lead us not into temptation;
But deliver us from evil.
Amen.

The following VERSICLES AND RESPONSES may then be
said by the Minister and People, except that at a funeral of a
child the first Versicle and Response shall not be said.

Minister   Enter not into judgement with thy servant,
             O Lord;
All   **For in thy sight shall no man living be justified.**

Minister   Grant unto *him* eternal rest;
All   **And let perpetual light shine upon *him*.**

Minister	We believe verily to see the goodness of the Lord;
All	**In the land of the living.**

Minister	O Lord, hear our prayer;
All	**And let our cry come unto thee.**

Then shall be said one or more of the following PRAYERS

Almighty God, with whom do live the spirits of them that depart hence in the Lord, and with whom the souls of the faithful, after they are delivered from the burden of the flesh, are in joy and felicity: We give thee hearty thanks, for that it hath pleased thee to deliver this our *brother* out of the miseries of this sinful world; beseeching thee, that it may please thee, of thy gracious goodness, shortly to accomplish the number of thine elect, and to hasten thy kingdom; that we, with all those that are departed in the true faith of thy holy name, may have our perfect consummation and bliss, both in body and soul, in thy eternal and everlasting glory; through Jesus Christ our Lord. **Amen.**

THE COLLECT

O merciful God, the Father of our Lord Jesus Christ, who is the resurrection and the life; in whom whosoever believeth shall live, though he die; and whosoever liveth, and believeth in him, shall not die eternally; who also hath taught us, by his holy Apostle Saint Paul, not to be sorry, as men without hope, for them that sleep in him: We meekly beseech thee, O Father, to raise us from the death of sin unto the life of righteousness; that, when we shall depart this life, we may rest in him, as our hope is this our *brother* doth; and that, at the general resurrection in the last day, we may be found acceptable in thy sight; and receive that blessing, which thy well-beloved Son shall then pronounce to all that love and fear thee, saying,

Come, ye blessed children of my Father, receive the kingdom prepared for you from the beginning of the world. Grant this, we beseech thee, O merciful Father, through Jesus Christ, our Mediator and Redeemer. **Amen.**

O Father of all, we pray to thee for those whom we love, but see no longer. Grant them thy peace; let light perpetual shine upon them; and in thy loving wisdom and almighty power work in them the good purpose of thy perfect will; through Jesus Christ our Lord. **Amen.**

Almighty God, Father of all mercies and giver of all comfort: Deal graciously, we pray thee, with those who mourn, that casting every care on thee, they may know the consolation of thy love; through Jesus Christ our Lord. **Amen.**

O heavenly Father, who in thy Son Jesus Christ, hast given us a true faith, and a sure hope: Help us, we pray thee, to live as those who believe and trust in the Communion of Saints, the forgiveness of sins, and the resurrection to life everlasting, and strengthen this faith and hope in us all the days of our life: through the love of thy Son, Jesus Christ our Saviour. **Amen.**

At the funeral of a child

O Lord Jesu Christ, who didst take little children into thine arms and bless them: Open thou our eyes, we beseech thee, to perceive that it is of thy goodness that thou hast taken this thy child into the everlasting arms of thine infinite love; who livest and reignest with the Father and the Holy Spirit, ever one God, world without end. **Amen.

O God, whose ways are hidden and thy works most wonderful, who makest nothing in vain and lovest all that thou hast made: Comfort thou thy servants, whose hearts are sore smitten and oppressed; and grant that they may so love and serve thee in this life, that together with this thy child, they may obtain the fulness of thy promises in the world to come; through Jesus Christ our Lord. **Amen.

The Committal follows. For a longer form of the Committal see page 68.

The Minister shall say

**Forasmuch as it hath pleased Almighty God of his great mercy to take unto himself the soul of our dear *brother* (or this *child*) here departed, we therefore commit *his* body to be consumed by fire (or to the ground); earth to earth, ashes to ashes, dust to dust; in sure and certain hope of the resurrection to eternal life through our Lord Jesus Christ; who shall change the body of our low estate that it may be like unto his glorious body, according to the mighty working, whereby he is able to subdue all things to himself.

Or this

We commend unto thy hands of mercy, most merciful Father, the soul of this our *brother* (or this thy *child*) departed, and we commit *his* body to be consumed by fire (or to the ground), earth to earth, ashes to ashes, dust to dust. And we beseech thine infinite goodness to give us grace to live in thy fear and love and to die in thy favour, that when the judgement shall come which thou hast committed to thy well-beloved Son, both this our *brother* (or this *child*) and we may be found acceptable in thy sight. Grant this, O merciful Father, for the sake of Jesus Christ, our only Saviour, Mediator, and Advocate. **Amen.

Then shall be said or sung

I heard a voice from heaven, saying unto me, Write, From henceforth blessed are the dead which die in the Lord: even so saith the Spirit; for they rest from their labours.

Or, at the funeral of a child

**They shall hunger no more, neither thirst any more; neither shall the sun light on them, nor any heat. For the Lamb which is in the midst of the throne shall feed them, and shall lead them unto living fountains of waters: and God shall wipe away all tears from their eyes.

Here may be added by the Minister

Now unto the King eternal, immortal, invisible, the only wise God, be honour and glory for ever and ever. **Amen.

or

The grace of our Lord Jesus Christ, and the love of God, and the fellowship of the Holy Ghost, be with us all evermore. **Amen.

The Committal

This Committal may be used before or after a Service in Church. The Minister shall say

Man that is born of a woman hath but a short time to live, and is full of misery. He cometh up, and is cut down, like a flower; he fleeth as it were a shadow, and never continueth in one stay.

In the midst of life we are in death: of whom may we seek for succour, but of thee, O Lord, who for our sins art justly displeased?

Yet, O Lord God most holy, O Lord most mighty, O holy and most merciful Saviour, deliver us not into the bitter pains of eternal death.

Thou knowest, Lord, the secrets of our hearts; shut not thy merciful ears to our prayer; but spare us, Lord most holy, O God most mighty, O holy and merciful Saviour, thou most worthy Judge eternal, suffer us not, at our last hour, for any pains of death, to fall from thee.

Or this

PSALM 103.13–17

Like as a father pitieth his own children:
even so is the Lord merciful unto them that fear him.

For he knoweth whereof we are made:
he remembereth that we are but dust.

The days of man are but as grass:
for he flourisheth as a flower in the field.

For as soon as the wind goeth over it, it is gone:
and the place thereof shall know it no more.

But the merciful goodness of the Lord
   endureth for ever and ever upon them that fear him:
and his righteousness upon children's children.

Then shall the Minister say

Forasmuch as it hath pleased Almighty God of his great mercy
to take unto himself the soul of our dear *brother* (or this *child*)
here departed, we therefore commit *his* body to be consumed
by fire (or to the ground); earth to earth, ashes to ashes, dust to
dust; in sure and certain hope of the resurrection to eternal life
through our Lord Jesus Christ; who shall change the body of
our low estate that it may be like unto his glorious body,
according to the mighty working, whereby he is able to subdue
all things to himself.

Or this

We commend unto thy hands of mercy, most merciful Father,
the soul of this our *brother* (or this thy *child*) departed, and we
commit *his* body to be consumed by fire (or to the ground),
earth to earth, ashes to ashes, dust to dust. And we beseech
thine infinite goodness to give us grace to live in thy fear and
love and to die in thy favour, that when the judgement shall
come which thou hast committed to thy well-beloved Son, both
this our *brother* (or this *child*) and we may be found acceptable
in thy sight. Grant this, O merciful Father, for the sake of Jesus
Christ, our only Saviour, Mediator, and Advocate. **Amen.**

Then shall be said or sung

I heard a voice from heaven, saying unto me, Write, From
henceforth blessed are the dead which die in the Lord: even so
saith the Spirit; for they rest from their labours.

Or, at the funeral of a child

**They shall hunger no more, neither thirst any more; neither shall the sun light on them, nor any heat. For the Lamb which is in the midst of the throne shall feed them, and shall lead them unto living fountains of waters: and God shall wipe away all tears from their eyes.

Here shall be added by the Minister

Now unto the King eternal, immortal, invisible, the only wise God, be honour and glory for ever and ever. **Amen.

or

The grace of our Lord Jesus Christ, and the love of God, and the fellowship of the Holy Ghost, be with us all evermore. **Amen.

Funeral Rites
The Roman Catholic Church

I Rite of Committal

WHEN A FUNERAL LITURGY HAS IMMEDIATELY PRECEDED

II Funeral Rite

WHEN NO OTHER LITURGY HAS TAKEN PLACE

I   Rite of Committal
The Roman Catholic Church

WHEN A FUNERAL LITURGY HAS IMMEDIATELY PRECEDED

INVITATION

The minister invites all to pray for the deceased. This may be followed by a hymn.

SCRIPTURE VERSE

PRAYER BEFORE COMMITTAL

COMMITTAL

INTERCESSIONS

One of the following responses concludes each petition:

> We pray to the Lord:
> **All:** **Lord, have mercy.**

or

> Lord, in your mercy.
> **All:** **Hear our prayer.**

or

> Lord, have mercy.
> **All:** **Lord, have mercy.**

THE LORD'S PRAYER

All: **Our Father, who art in heaven,
hallowed be thy name.
Thy kingdom come.
Thy will be done on earth, as it is in heaven.
Give us this day our daily bread,
and forgive us our trespasses,
as we forgive those who trespass against us,
and lead us not into temptation
but deliver us from evil.**

CONCLUDING PRAYER

PRAYER OVER THE PEOPLE

After the prayer the following is said:

Eternal rest grant unto him/her, O Lord.
All: **And let perpetual light shine upon him/her.**

May he/she rest in peace.
All: **Amen.**

May his/her soul and the souls of all the faithful departed,
through the mercy of God, rest in peace.
All: **Amen.**

BLESSING

DISMISSAL

Go in peace of Christ.
All: **Thanks be to God.**

A concluding hymn may be sung.

II Funeral Rite
The Roman Catholic Church

WHEN NO OTHER LITURGY HAS TAKEN PLACE

INTRODUCTORY RITES

GREETING

The minister greets the people and all reply:

All: **And also with you.**

SPRINKLING WITH HOLY WATER

The coffin is sprinkled with Holy Water as a reminder of baptism.

PLACING OF CHRISTIAN SYMBOLS

OPENING PRAYER

LITURGY OF THE WORD

SCRIPTURE READING
All sit.
At the end of the reading:

This is the Word of the Lord.
All: **Thanks be to God.**

PSALM

[SCRIPTURE READING]

GOSPEL READING
All stand.

> The Lord be with you.

All: **And also with you.**

> A reading from the holy Gospel according to ...

All: **Glory to you, Lord.**

At the end of the Gospel:

> This is the Gospel of the Lord.

All: **Praise to you, Lord Jesus Christ.**

HOMILY
All sit.

INTERCESSIONS
All stand.

One of the following responses concludes each petition:

> Lord, in your mercy.

All: **Hear our prayer.**

or

> We pray to the Lord:

All: **Lord, hear our prayer.**

THE LORD'S PRAYER

All: **Our Father, who art in heaven,**
hallowed be thy name.
Thy kingdom come.
Thy will be done on earth, as it is in heaven.
Give us this day our daily bread,
and forgive us our trespasses,
as we forgive those who trespass against us,
and lead us not into temptation
but deliver us from evil.

CONCLUDING PRAYER

FINAL COMMENDATION

[WORDS IN REMEMBRANCE]

A member or a friend of the family may speak in remembrance of the deceased.

INVITATION TO PRAYER

SPRINKLING WITH HOLY WATER

SONG OF FAREWELL

One of the following, or another suitable hymn is used:

A   I know that my redeemer lives,
And on that final day of days,
His voice shall bid me rise again:
Unending joy, unceasing praise!

This hope I cherish in my heart
To stand on earth, my flesh restored
And, not a stranger but a friend,
Behold my Saviour and my Lord.

or

B   Saints of God, come to his/her aid!
Hasten to meet him/her, angels of the Lord!

All: **Receive his/her soul and present him/her
to God the Most High.**

May Christ, who called you, take you to himself;
may angels lead you to the bosom of Abraham.

All: **Receive his/her soul and present him/her
to God the Most High.**

Eternal rest grant unto him/her, O Lord,
and let perpetual light shine upon him/her.

All: **Receive his/her soul and present him/her
to God the Most High.**

76

PRAYER OF COMMENDATION AND THE COMMITTAL

CONCLUDING RITE

PRAYER OVER THE PEOPLE

After the prayer the following is said:

> Eternal rest grant unto him/her, O Lord.

All: **And let perpetual light shine upon him/her.**

> May he/she rest in peace.

All: **Amen.**

> May his/her soul and the souls of all the faithful departed, through the mercy of God, rest in peace.

All: **Amen.**

BLESSING

DISMISSAL

> Go in the peace of Christ.

All: **Thanks be to God.**

A concluding hymn may be sung.

PSALM 121

I lift up my eyes to the hills:
but where shall I find help?

My help comes from the Lord:
who has made heaven and earth.

He will not suffer your foot to stumble:
and he who watches over you will not sleep.

Be sure he who has charge of Israel:
will neither slumber nor sleep.

The Lord himself is your keeper:
the Lord is your defence upon your right hand;

The sun shall not strike you by day:
nor shall the moon by night.

The Lord will defend you from all evil:
it is he who will guard your life.

The Lord will defend your going out and your coming in:
from this time forward for evermore.

A Selection of 44 Hymns

*Verses preceded by an * may be omitted*

The words of the hymn 'God be in my head' can be found on page 38 in the Church of England (Common Worship) Funeral Service.

1 ABIDE with me; fast falls the eventide;
   the darkness deepens; Lord, with me abide!
   when other helpers fail, and comforts flee,
   help of the helpless, O abide with me.

2 Swift to its close ebbs out life's little day;
   earth's joys grow dim, its glories pass away;
   change and decay in all around I see;
   O thou who changest not, abide with me.

3 I need thy presence every passing hour;
   what but thy grace can foil the tempter's power?
   who like thyself my guide and stay can be?
   through cloud and sunshine, O abide with me.

4 I fear no foe with thee at hand to bless;
   ills have no weight, and tears no bitterness.
   Where is death's sting? Where, grave, thy victory?
   I triumph still, if thou abide with me.

5 Hold thou thy cross before my closing eyes;
   shine through the gloom, and point me to the skies:
   Heaven's morning breaks, and earth's vain shadows flee;
   in life, in death, O Lord, abide with me!

1 *ALL things bright and beautiful,*
    all creatures great and small,
all things wise and wonderful,
    the Lord God made them all.

2 Each little flower that opens,
    each little bird that sings,
he made their glowing colours,
    he made their tiny wings:

3 The purple-headed mountain,
    the river running by,
the sunset, and the morning
    that brightens up the sky:

4 The cold wind in the winter,
    the pleasant summer sun,
the ripe fruits in the garden,
    he made them every one:

*5 The tall trees in the greenwood,
    the meadows where we play,
the rushes by the water
    we gather every day:

6 He gave us eyes to see them,
    and lips that we might tell
how great is God almighty,
    who has made all things well:

7 *ALL things bright and beautiful,*
    all creatures great and small,
all things wise and wonderful,
    the Lord God made them all.

80

1 ALLELUIA, sing to Jesus!
   his the sceptre, his the throne;
alleluia, his the triumph,
   his the victory alone:
hark, the songs of peaceful Sion
   thunder like a mighty flood;
Jesus out of every nation
   hath redeemed us by his blood.

2 Alleluia, not as orphans
   are we left in sorrow now;
alleluia, he is near us,
   faith believes, nor questions how:
though the cloud from sight received him,
   when the forty days were o'er,
shall our hearts forget his promise,
   'I am with you evermore'?

3 Alleluia, bread of angels,
   thou on earth our food, our stay;
alleluia, here the sinful
   flee to thee from day to day:
Intercessor, Friend of sinners,
   earth's Redeemer, plead for me,
where the songs of all the sinless
   sweep across the crystal sea.

4 Alleluia, King eternal,
   thee the Lord of lords we own;
alleluia, born of Mary,
   earth thy footstool, heaven thy throne:
thou within the veil hast entered,
   robed in flesh, our great High Priest;
thou on earth both Priest and Victim
   in the eucharistic feast.

1 AMAZING grace (how sweet the sound)
   that saved a wretch like me!
I once was lost, but now am found,
   was blind, but now I see.

2 'Twas grace that taught my heart to fear,
   and grace my fears relieved;
how precious did that grace appear
   the hour I first believed!

3 Through many dangers, toils and snares
   I have already come:
'tis grace has brought me safe thus far,
   and grace will lead me home.

4 The Lord has promised good to me,
   his word my hope secures;
he will my shield and portion be
   as long as life endures.

5 Yes, when this flesh and heart shall fail,
   and mortal life shall cease:
I shall possess, within the veil,
   a life of joy and peace.

6 When we've been there ten thousand years,
   bright shining as the sun,
we've no less days to sing God's praise,
   than when we first begun.

1 AND did those feet in ancient time
    walk upon England's mountains green?
And was the holy Lamb of God
    on England's pleasant pastures seen?
And did the countenance divine
    shine forth upon our clouded hills?
And was Jerusalem builded here
    among these dark satanic mills?

2 Bring me my bow of burning gold!
    Bring me my arrows of desire!
Bring me my spear! O clouds, unfold!
    Bring me my chariot of fire!
I will not cease from mental fight,
    nor shall my sword sleep in my hand,
till we have built Jerusalem
    in England's green and pleasant land.

1 BE still, my soul: the Lord is on your side;
       bear patiently the cross of grief and pain;
   leave to your God to order and provide;
       in every change he faithful will remain.
   Be still, my soul: your best, your heavenly friend
   through thorny ways leads to a joyful end.

2 Be still, my soul: your God will undertake
       to guide the future as he has the past.
   Your hope, your confidence let nothing shake,
       all now mysterious shall be clear at last.
   Be still, my soul: the waves and winds still know
   his voice, who ruled them while he dwelt below.

3 Be still, my soul: when dearest friends depart
       and all is darkened in the vale of tears,
   then you shall better know his love, his heart,
       who comes to soothe your sorrow, calm your fears.
   Be still, my soul: for Jesus can repay
   from his own fullness all he takes away.

4 Be still, my soul: the hour is hastening on
       when we shall be for ever with the Lord,
   when disappointment, grief and fear are gone,
       sorrow forgotten, love's pure joy restored.
   Be still, my soul: when change and tears are past,
   all safe and blessed we shall meet at last.

1   BLEST are the pure in heart,
       for they shall see our God;
  the secret of the Lord is theirs,
       their soul is Christ's abode.

2   The Lord, who left the heavens
       our life and peace to bring,
  to dwell in lowliness with men,
       their pattern and their King;

3   Still to the lowly soul
       he doth himself impart,
  and for his dwelling and his throne
       chooseth the pure in heart.

4   Lord, we thy presence seek;
       may ours this blessing be;
  give us a pure and lowly heart,
       a temple meet for thee.

1 DEAR Lord and Father of mankind,
forgive our foolish ways;
re-clothe us in our rightful mind,
in purer lives thy service find,
in deeper reverence praise.

2 In simple trust like theirs who heard,
beside the Syrian sea,
the gracious calling of the Lord,
let us, like them, without a word
rise up and follow thee.

*3 O Sabbath rest by Galilee!
O calm of hills above,
where Jesus knelt to share with thee
the silence of eternity,
interpreted by love!

4 Drop thy still dews of quietness,
till all our strivings cease;
take from our souls the strain and stress,
and let our ordered lives confess
the beauty of thy peace.

5 Breathe through the heats of our desire
thy coolness and thy balm;
let sense be dumb, let flesh retire;
speak through the earthquake, wind, and fire,
O still small voice of calm.

1 ETERNAL Father, strong to save,
  whose arm hath bound the restless wave,
  who bidd'st the mighty ocean deep
  its own appointed limits keep:
    O hear us when we cry to thee
    for those in peril on the sea.

2 O Christ, whose voice the waters heard
  and hushed their raging at thy word,
  who walkedst on the foaming deep,
  and calm amid the storm didst sleep:
    O hear us when we cry to thee
    for those in peril on the sea.

3 O Holy Spirit, who didst brood
  upon the waters dark and rude,
  and bid their angry tumult cease,
  and give, for wild confusion, peace:
    O hear us when we cry to thee
    for those in peril on the sea.

4 O Trinity of love and power,
  our brethren shield in danger's hour;
  from rock and tempest, fire and foe,
  protect them wheresoe'er they go:
    thus evermore shall rise to thee
    glad hymns of praise from land and sea.

1 FOR all the saints who from their labours rest,
  who thee by faith before the world confessed,
  thy name, O Jesu, be for ever blest.
    Alleluia.

2 Thou wast their rock, their fortress, and their might;
  thou, Lord, their Captain in the well-fought fight;
  thou, in the darkness, still their one true light.
    Alleluia.

3 O may thy soldiers, faithful, true, and bold,
  fight as the saints who nobly fought of old,
  and win, with them, the victor's crown of gold.
    Alleluia.

4 O blest communion, fellowship divine!
  we feebly struggle, they in glory shine;
  yet all are one in thee, for all are thine.
    Alleluia.

5 And when the strife is fierce, the warfare long,
  steals on the ear the distant triumph-song,
  and hearts are brave again, and arms are strong.
    Alleluia.

6 The golden evening brightens in the west;
  soon, soon to faithful warriors comes their rest:
  sweet is the calm of paradise the blest.
    Alleluia.

7 But lo, there breaks a yet more glorious day;
   the saints triumphant rise in bright array;
   the King of glory passes on his way.
      Alleluia.

8 From earth's wide bounds, from ocean's farthest coast,
   through gates of pearl streams in the countless host,
   singing to Father, Son, and Holy Ghost.
      Alleluia.

1 GREAT is thy faithfulness, O God my Father,
    there is no shadow of turning with thee;
thou changest not, thy compassions they fail not;
    as thou hast been thou for ever wilt be:
    Great is thy faithfulness! Great is thy faithfulness!
    Morning by morning new mercies I see;
    all I have needed thy hand has provided,
    great is thy faithfulness, Lord, unto me.

2 Summer and winter, and springtime and harvest,
    sun, moon and stars in their courses above,
join with all nature in manifold witness
    to thy great faithfulness, mercy and love:

3 Pardon for sin and a peace that endureth,
    thy own dear presence to cheer and to guide;
strength for today and bright hope for tomorrow,
    blessings all mine, with ten thousand beside!

1 GUIDE me, O thou great Redeemer,
    pilgrim through this barren land;
I am weak, but thou art mighty;
    hold me with thy powerful hand:
      Bread of heaven,
    feed me now and evermore.

2 Open now the crystal fountain
    whence the healing stream doth flow;
let the fiery cloudy pillar
    lead me all my journey through:
      strong deliverer,
    be thou still my strength and shield.

3 When I tread the verge of Jordan,
    bid my anxious fears subside;
death of death, and hell's destruction,
    land me safe on Canaan's side:
      songs and praises
    I will ever give to thee.

1 HOW sweet the name of Jesus sounds
    in a believer's ear!
It soothes his sorrows, heals his wounds,
    and drives away his fear.

2 It makes the wounded spirit whole,
    and calms the troubled breast;
'tis manna to the hungry soul,
    and to the weary rest.

3 Dear name! the rock on which I build,
    my shield and hiding-place,
my never-failing treasury filled
    with boundless stores of grace.

4 Jesus! my Shepherd, Brother, Friend,
    my Prophet, Priest, and King,
my Lord, my Life, my Way, my End,
    accept the praise I bring.

5 Weak is the effort of my heart,
    and cold my warmest thought;
but when I see thee as thou art,
    I'll praise thee as I ought.

6 Till then I would thy love proclaim
    with every fleeting breath;
and may the music of thy name
    refresh my soul in death.

1 I AM the Bread of Life.
   You who come to Me shall not hunger:
   And who believe in Me shall not thirst.
   No one can come to Me unless the
   Father beckons.
   And I will raise you up,
   And I will raise you up,
   And I will raise you up,
   On the last day.

2 The bread that I will give
   Is My flesh for the life of the world;
   And if you eat of this bread,
   You shall live for ever
   You shall live for ever.
   And I will raise ...

3 Unless you eat
   Of the flesh of the Son of Man
   And drink of His blood,
   And drink of His blood,
   You shall not have life within you.
   And I will raise ...

4 I am the Resurrection,
   I am the Life;
   If you believe in Me,
   Even though you die, you shall live for ever.
   And I will raise ...

5 Yes, Lord, I believe
   That You are the Christ,
   The Son of God,
   Who has come into the world.
   And I will raise ...

1 I HEARD the voice of Jesus say,
    'Come unto me and rest;
lay down, thou weary one, lay down
    thy head upon my breast':
I came to Jesus as I was,
    weary and worn and sad;
I found in him a resting-place,
    and he has made me glad.

2 I heard the voice of Jesus say,
    'Behold, I freely give
the living water, thirsty one;
    stoop down and drink and live':
I came to Jesus, and I drank
    of that life-giving stream;
my thirst was quenched, my soul revived,
    and now I live in him.

3 I heard the voice of Jesus say,
    'I am this dark world's light;
look unto me, thy morn shall rise,
    and all thy day be bright':
I looked to Jesus, and I found
    in him my star, my sun;
and in that light of life I'll walk
    till travelling days are done.

1 IMMORTAL, invisible, God only wise,
   in light inaccessible hid from our eyes,
   most blessed, most glorious, the Ancient of Days,
   almighty, victorious, thy great name we praise.

2 Unresting, unhasting, and silent as light,
   nor wanting, nor wasting, thou rulest in might;
   thy justice like mountains high soaring above
   thy clouds which are fountains of goodness and love.

3 To all life thou givest, to both great and small;
   in all life thou livest, the true life of all;
   we blossom and flourish as leaves on the tree,
   and wither and perish; but naught changeth thee.

4 Great Father of glory, pure Father of light,
   thine angels adore thee, all veiling their sight;
   all laud we would render: O help us to see
   'tis only the splendour of light hideth thee.

1 IN heavenly love abiding,
    no change my heart shall fear;
    and safe is such confiding,
    for nothing changes here:
    the storm may roar without me,
    my heart may low be laid;
    but God is round about me,
    and can I be dismayed?

2 Wherever he may guide me,
    no want shall turn me back;
    my Shepherd is beside me,
    and nothing can I lack:
    his wisdom ever waketh,
    his sight is never dim,
    he knows the way he taketh,
    and I will walk with him.

3 Green pastures are before me,
    which yet I have not seen;
    bright skies will soon be o'er me,
    where darkest clouds have been;
    my hope I cannot measure,
    my path to life is free;
    my Saviour has my treasure,
    and he will walk with me.

1   JESUS lives! thy terrors now
can, O death, no more appal us;
    Jesus lives! by this we know
thou, O grave, canst not enthral us.
    Alleluia.

2   Jesus lives! henceforth is death
but the gate of life immortal:
    this shall calm our trembling breath,
when we pass its gloomy portal.
    Alleluia.

3   Jesus lives! for us he died;
then, alone to Jesus living,
    pure in heart may we abide,
glory to our Saviour giving.
    Alleluia.

4   Jesus lives! our hearts know well
naught from us his love shall sever;
    life nor death nor powers of hell
tear us from his keeping ever.
    Alleluia.

5   Jesus lives! to him the throne
over all the world is given:
    may we go where he is gone,
rest and reign with him in heaven.
    Alleluia.

1 JESU, lover of my soul,
    let me to thy bosom fly,
while the nearer waters roll,
    while the tempest still is high:
hide me, O my Saviour, hide,
    till the storm of life is past;
safe into the haven guide,
    O receive my soul at last.

2 Other refuge have I none,
    hangs my helpless soul on thee;
leave, ah, leave me not alone,
    still support and comfort me.
All my trust on thee is stayed,
    all my help from thee I bring;
cover my defenceless head
    with the shadow of thy wing.

3 Thou, O Christ, art all I want;
    more than all in thee I find;
raise the fallen, cheer the faint,
    heal the sick, and lead the blind.
Just and holy is thy name,
    I am all unrighteousness;
false and full of sin I am,
    thou art full of truth and grace.

4 Plenteous grace with thee is found,
    grace to cover all my sin;
let the healing streams abound,
    make and keep me pure within.
Thou of life the fountain art:
    freely let me take of thee,
spring thou up within my heart,
    rise to all eternity.

1 JUST as I am, without one plea
  but that thy blood was shed for me,
  and that thou bidst me come to thee,
    O Lamb of God, I come.

2 Just as I am, though tossed about
  with many a conflict, many a doubt,
  fightings and fears within, without,
    O Lamb of God, I come.

3 Just as I am, poor, wretched, blind;
  sight, riches, healing of the mind,
  yea, all I need, in thee to find,
    O Lamb of God, I come.

4 Just as I am, thou wilt receive,
  wilt welcome, pardon, cleanse, relieve:
  because thy promise I believe,
    O Lamb of God, I come.

5 Just as I am, thy love unknown
  has broken every barrier down;
  now to be thine, yea, thine alone,
    O Lamb of God, I come.

6 Just as I am, of that free love
  the breadth, length, depth, and height to prove,
  here for a season, then above,
    O Lamb of God, I come.

1 LEAD us, heavenly Father, lead us
      o'er the world's tempestuous sea;
   guard us, guide us, keep us, feed us,
      for we have no help but thee;
   yet possessing every blessing,
      if our God our Father be.

2 Saviour, breathe forgiveness o'er
   us:
      all our weakness thou dost know;
   thou didst tread this earth before
   us,
      thou didst feel its keenest woe;
   lone and dreary, faint and weary,
      through the desert thou didst go.

3 Spirit of our God, descending,
      fill our hearts with heavenly joy,
   love with every passion blending,
      pleasure that can never cloy:
   thus provided, pardoned, guided,
      nothing can our peace destroy.

1 LORD of all hopefulness, Lord of all joy,
   whose trust, ever childlike, no cares could destroy,
   be there at our waking, and give us, we pray,
   your bliss in our hearts, Lord, at the break of the day.

2 Lord of all eagerness, Lord of all faith,
   whose strong hands were skilled at the plane and the lathe,
   be there at our labours, and give us, we pray,
   your strength in our hearts, Lord, at the noon of the day.

3 Lord of all kindliness, Lord of all grace,
   your hands swift to welcome, your arms to embrace,
   be there at our homing, and give us, we pray,
   your love in our hearts, Lord, at the eve of the day.

4 Lord of all gentleness, Lord of all calm,
   whose voice is contentment, whose presence is balm,
   be there at our sleeping, and give us, we pray,
   your peace in our hearts, Lord, at the end of the day.

1 LOVE divine, all loves excelling,
    joy of heaven, to earth come down,
fix in us thy humble dwelling,
    all thy faithful mercies crown.
Jesu, thou art all compassion,
    pure unbounded love thou art;
visit us with thy salvation,
    enter every trembling heart.

2 Come, almighty to deliver,
    let us all thy grace receive;
suddenly return, and never,
    never more thy temples leave.
Thee we would be always blessing,
    serve thee as thy hosts above;
pray, and praise thee, without ceasing,
    glory in thy perfect love.

3 Finish then thy new creation:
    pure and spotless let us be;
let us see thy great salvation
    perfectly restored in thee;
changed from glory into glory
    till in heaven we take our place,
till we cast our crowns before thee,
    lost in wonder, love, and praise.

1 LOVE'S redeeming work is done;
  fought the fight, the battle won:
  lo, our Sun's eclipse is o'er,
  lo, he sets in blood no more.

2 Vain the stone, the watch, the seal;
  Christ has burst the gates of hell;
  death in vain forbids his rise;
  Christ has opened paradise.

3 Lives again our glorious King;
  where, O death, is now thy sting?
  dying once, he all doth save;
  where thy victory, O grave?

4 Soar we now where Christ has
  led,
  following our exalted Head;
  made like him, like him we rise;
  ours the cross, the grave, the skies.

5 Hail the Lord of earth and
  heaven!
  Praise to thee by both be given:
  thee we greet triumphant now;
  hail, the Resurrection Thou!

1 MAKE me a channel of your peace.
Where there is hatred, let me bring your love;
where there is injury, your pardon, Lord;
and where there's doubt, true faith in you.
O Master, grant that I may never seek
so much to be consoled as to console,
to be understood as to understand,
to be loved, as to love with all my soul.

2 Make me a channel of your peace.
Where there's despair in life, let me bring hope;
where there is darkness, only light;
and where there's sadness, ever joy.
O Master, grant that I may never seek
so much to be consoled as to console,
to be understood as to understand,
to be loved, as to love with all my soul.

3 Make me a channel of your peace.
It is in pardoning that we are pardoned,
in giving to all men that we receive,
and in dying that we're born to eternal life.

1 MORNING has broken, like the first morning;
    blackbird has spoken, like the first bird.
  Praise for the singing! Praise for the morning!
    Praise for them, springing fresh from the Word!

2 Sweet the rain's new fall sunlit from heaven,
    like the first dewfall on the first grass.
  Praise for the sweetness of the wet garden,
    sprung in completeness where his feet pass.

3 Mine is the sunlight! Mine is the morning
    born of the one light Eden saw play!
  Praise with elation, praise every morning,
    God's re-creation of the new day!

1   NOW thank we all our God
with heart and hands and voices,
    who wondrous things hath done,
in whom his world rejoices;
    who from our mother's arms
        hath blessed us on our way
    with countless gifts of love,
        and still is ours to-day.

2   O may this bounteous God
through all our life be near us,
    with ever joyful hearts
and blessed peace to cheer us;
    and keep us in his grace,
        and guide us when perplexed,
    and free us from all ills
        in this world and the next.

3   All praise and thanks to God
the Father now be given,
    the Son, and him who reigns
with them in highest heaven,
    the one eternal God,
        whom earth and heaven adore;
    for thus it was, is now,
        and shall be evermore.

1 O GOD, our help in ages past,
    our hope for years to come,
  our shelter from the stormy blast,
    and our eternal home;

2 Under the shadow of thy throne
    thy saints have dwelt secure;
  sufficient is thine arm alone,
    and our defence is sure.

3 Before the hills in order stood,
    or earth received her frame,
  from everlasting thou art God,
    to endless years the same.

4 A thousand ages in thy sight
    are like an evening gone,
  short as the watch that ends the night
    before the rising sun.

5 Time, like an ever-rolling stream,
    bears all its sons away;
  they fly forgotten, as a dream
    dies at the opening day.

6 O God, our help in ages past,
    our hope for years to come,
  be thou our guard while troubles last,
    and our eternal home.

1 O JESUS, I have promised
    to serve thee to the end;
be thou for ever near me,
    my Master and my Friend:
I shall not fear the battle
    if thou art by my side,
nor wander from the pathway
    if thou wilt be my guide.

2 O let me feel thee near me:
    the world is ever near;
I see the sights that dazzle,
    the tempting sounds I hear;
my foes are ever near me,
    around me and within;
but, Jesus, draw thou nearer,
    and shield my soul from sin.

3 O let me hear thee speaking
    in accents clear and still
above the storms of passion,
    the murmurs of self-will;
O speak to reassure me,
    to hasten or control;
O speak, and make me listen,
    thou guardian of my soul.

4 O Jesus, thou hast promised
    to all who follow thee,
  that where thou art in glory
    there shall thy servant be;
  and, Jesus, I have promised
    to serve thee to the end:
  O give me grace to follow,
    my Master and my Friend.

5 O let me see thy foot-marks,
    and in them plant mine own;
  my hope to follow duly
    is in thy strength alone:
  O guide me, call me, draw me,
    uphold me to the end;
  and then in heaven receive me,
    my Saviour and my Friend.

1 O LORD my God, when I in awesome wonder
   consider all the works thy hand hath made,
I see the stars, I hear the mighty thunder,
   thy power throughout the universe displayed;
   Then sings my soul, my Saviour God, to thee,
      how great thou art, how great thou art!
   Then sings my soul, my Saviour God, to thee,
      how great thou art, how great thou art!

2 When through the woods and forest glades I wander,
   and hear the birds sing sweetly in the trees;
when I look down from lofty mountain grandeur,
   and hear the brook, and feel the gentle breeze;
   Then sings my soul, ...

3 And when I think that God, his Son not sparing,
   sent him to die — I scarce can take it in:
that on the cross, my burden gladly bearing,
   he bled and died to take away my sin;
   Then sings my soul, ...

4 When Christ shall come with shout of acclamation
   and take me home — what joy shall fill my heart!
Then shall I bow in humble adoration,
   and there proclaim, my God, how great thou art!
   Then sings my soul, my Saviour God, to thee,
      how great thou art, how great thou art!
   Then sings my soul, my Saviour God, to thee,
      how great thou art, how great thou art!

1 O LOVE that wilt not let me go,
     I rest my weary soul in thee;
   I give thee back the life I owe,
   that in thine ocean depths its flow
     may richer, fuller be.

2 O light that followest all my way,
     I yield my flickering torch to thee;
   my heart restores its borrowed ray,
   that in thy sunshine's blaze its day
     may brighter, fairer be.

3 O joy that seekest me through pain,
     I cannot close my heart to thee;
   I trace the rainbow through the rain,
   and feel the promise is not vain,
     that morn shall tearless be.

4 O cross that liftest up my head,
     I dare not ask to fly from thee;
   I lay in dust life's glory dead,
   and from the ground there blossoms red
     life that shall endless be.

1 ON a hill far away stood an old rugged cross,
   The emblem of suff'ring and shame;
   And I loved that old cross where the dearest and best
   For a world of lost sinners was slain.

   So I'll cherish the old rugged cross,
   Till my trophies at last I lay down;
   I will cling to the old rugged cross
   And exchange it someday for a crown.

2 Oh that old rugged cross, so despised by the world,
   Has a wondrous attraction for me:
   For the dear Lamb of God left his glory above
   To bear it to dark Calvary.

   So I'll cherish the old rugged cross,

3 In the old rugged cross, stained with blood so divine,
   A wondrous beauty I see.
   For 'twas on that old cross Jesus suffered and died
   To pardon and sanctify me.

   So I'll cherish the old rugged cross,

4 To the old rugged cross I will ever be true,
   Its shame and reproach gladly bear.
   Then he'll call me some day to my home far away,
   There his glory for ever I'll share.

   So I'll cherish the old rugged cross,

1 PEACE, perfect peace, in this dark world of sin?
   The blood of Jesus whispers peace within.

2 Peace, perfect peace, by thronging duties pressed?
   To do the will of Jesus, this is rest.

3 Peace, perfect peace, death shadowing us and ours?
   Jesus has vanquished death and all its powers.

4 Peace, perfect peace, our future all unknown?
   Jesus we know, and he is on the throne.

5 It is enough: earth's struggles soon shall cease,
   and Jesus call to heaven's perfect peace.

1 PRAISE, my soul, the King of heaven,
   to his feet thy tribute bring;
ransomed, healed, restored, forgiven,
   who like me his praise should sing?
     Alleluia, alleluia,
   praise the everlasting King.

2 Praise him for his grace and favour
   to our fathers in distress;
praise him still the same for ever,
   slow to chide, and swift to bless:
     Alleluia, alleluia,
   glorious in his faithfulness.

3 Father-like, he tends and spares us,
   well our feeble frame he knows;
in his hands he gently bears us,
   rescues us from all our foes:
     Alleluia, alleluia,
   widely as his mercy flows.

4 Angels, help us to adore him;
   ye behold him face to face;
sun and moon, bow down before him,
   dwellers all in time and space:
     Alleluia, alleluia,
   praise with us the God of grace.

1 ROCK of ages, cleft for me,
   let me hide myself in thee;
   let the water and the blood,
   from thy riven side which flowed,
   be of sin the double cure:
   cleanse me from its guilt and power.

2 Not the labours of my hands
   can fulfil thy law's demands;
   could my zeal no respite know,
   could my tears for ever flow,
   all for sin could not atone:
   thou must save, and thou alone.

3 Nothing in my hand I bring,
   simply to thy cross I cling;
   naked, come to thee for dress;
   helpless, look to thee for grace;
   foul, I to the fountain fly;
   wash me, Saviour, or I die.

4 While I draw this fleeting breath,
   when my eyelids close in death,
   when I soar through tracts unknown,
   see thee on thy judgement throne;
   Rock of ages, cleft for me,
   let me hide myself in thee.

1 THE day thou gavest, Lord, is ended,
  the darkness falls at thy behest;
 to thee our morning hymns ascended,
  thy praise shall sanctify our rest.

2 We thank thee that thy Church unsleeping,
  while earth rolls onward into light,
 through all the world her watch is keeping,
  and rests not now by day or night.

3 As o'er each continent and island
  the dawn leads on another day,
 the voice of prayer is never silent,
  nor dies the strain of praise away.

4 The sun that bids us rest is waking
  our brethren 'neath the western sky,
 and hour by hour fresh lips are making
  thy wondrous doings heard on high.

5 So be it, Lord: thy throne shall never,
  like earth's proud empires, pass away;
 thy kingdom stands, and grows for ever,
  till all thy creatures own thy sway.

1 THE King of love my shepherd is,
　　whose goodness faileth never;
I nothing lack if I am his
　　and he is mine for ever.

2 Where streams of living water flow
　　my ransomed soul he leadeth,
and where the verdant pastures grow
　　with food celestial feedeth.

3 Perverse and foolish oft I strayed,
　　but yet in love he sought me,
and on his shoulder gently laid,
　　and home rejoicing brought me.

4 In death's dark vale I fear no ill
　　with thee, dear Lord, beside me;
thy rod and staff my comfort still,
　　thy cross before to guide me.

5 Thou spread'st a table in my sight;
　　thy unction grace bestoweth;
and O what transport of delight
　　from thy pure chalice floweth!

6 And so through all the length of days
　　thy goodness faileth never:
good Shepherd, may I sing thy praise
　　within thy house for ever.

1 THE Lord's my Shepherd, I'll not want;
    he makes me down to lie
in pastures green; he leadeth me
    the quiet waters by.

2 My soul he doth restore again,
    and me to walk doth make
within the paths of righteousness,
    e'en for his own name's sake.

3 Yea, though I walk through death's dark vale,
    yet will I fear none ill;
for thou art with me, and thy rod
    and staff me comfort still.

4 My table thou hast furnished
    in presence of my foes;
my head thou dost with oil anoint,
    and my cup overflows.

5 Goodness and mercy all my life
    shall surely follow me;
and in God's house for evermore
    my dwelling-place shall be.

1 THE strife is o'er, the battle done;
  now is the Victor's triumph won;
  O let the song of praise be sung:
      Alleluia.

2 Death's mightiest powers have done their worst,
  and Jesus hath his foes dispersed;
  let shouts of praise and joy outburst:
      Alleluia.

3 On the third morn he rose again
  glorious in majesty to reign;
  O let us swell the joyful strain:
      Alleluia.

4 Lord, by the stripes which wounded thee
  from death's dread sting thy servants free,
  that we may live, and sing to thee
      Alleluia.

1 THERE is a green hill far away,
    without a city wall,
  where the dear Lord was crucified,
    who died to save us all.

2 We may not know, we cannot tell,
    what pains he had to bear,
  but we believe it was for us
    he hung and suffered there.

3 He died that we might be forgiven,
    he died to make us good,
  that we might go at last to heaven,
    saved by his precious blood.

4 There was no other good enough
    to pay the price of sin;
  he only could unlock the gate
    of heaven, and let us in.

5 O dearly, dearly has he loved,
    and we must love him too,
  and trust in his redeeming blood,
    and try his works to do.

1 THERE is a Redeemer,
   Jesus, God's own Son,
   Precious Lamb of God, Messiah,
   Holy One.

   Thank You, O my Father
   For giving us Your Son,
   And leaving Your Spirit
   Till the work on earth is done.

2 Jesus my Redeemer,
   Name above all names,
   Precious Lamb of God, Messiah,
   O for sinners slain:

   Thank You ...

3 When I stand in glory
   I will see His face,
   And there I'll serve my King for ever
   In that holy place.

   Thank You ...

1   THINE be the glory, risen, conquering Son,
endless is the victory thou o'er death hast won;
angels in bright raiment rolled the stone away,
kept the folded grave-clothes where thy body lay.
Thine be the glory, risen, conquering Son,
endless is the victory thou o'er death hast won.

2   Lo, Jesus meets us, risen from the tomb;
lovingly he greets us, scatters fear and gloom;
let the church with gladness hymns of triumph sing,
for her Lord now liveth, death hath lost its sting:
Thine be the glory ...

3   No more we doubt thee, glorious Prince of Life;
life is naught without thee: aid us in our strife;
make us more than conquerors through thy deathless love;
bring us safe through Jordan to thy home above:
Thine be the glory, risen, conquering Son,
endless is the victory thou o'er death hast won.

1 TO God be the glory, great things he has done!
   So loved he the world that he gave us his Son,
   who yielded his life an atonement for sin
   and opened the life-gate that all may go in.
   Praise the Lord! Praise the Lord!
     Let the earth hear his voice!
   Praise the Lord! Praise the Lord!
     Let the people rejoice!
   O come to the Father, through Jesus the Son,
   and give him the glory! Great things he has done!

2 O perfect redemption, the purchase of blood!
   To every believer the promise of God!
   The vilest offender who truly believes,
   that moment from Jesus forgiveness receives.
   Praise the Lord! ...

3 Great things he has taught us, great things he has done,
   and great our rejoicing through Jesus the Son;
   but purer and higher and greater will be
   our wonder, our rapture, when Jesus we see.
   Praise the Lord! ...

1 WHEN I survey the wondrous cross
        on which the Prince of glory died,
    my richest gain I count but loss,
        and pour contempt on all my pride.

2 Forbid it, Lord, that I should boast
        save in the cross of Christ my God;
    all the vain things that charm me most,
        I sacrifice them to his blood.

3 See from his head, his hands, his feet,
        sorrow and love flow mingled down;
    did e'er such love and sorrow meet,
        or thorns compose so rich a crown!

4 His dying crimson, like a robe,
        spreads o'er his body on the tree:
    then am I dead to all the globe,
        and all the globe is dead to me.

5 Were the whole realm of nature mine,
        that were a present far too small;
    love so amazing, so divine,
        demands my soul, my life, my all.

Index to Hymns

Index to Psalms and Canticles

Sources and Acknowledgements

The Origins of this Book

The Churches' Group (formerly Joint Group) on Funeral Services at Cemeteries and Crematoria, the membership of which is set out on page iv, sponsored in 1985 an ecumenical handbook *Funerals and Ministry to the Bereaved* intended for the use of clergy, funeral directors and crematoria and cemetery staff. During the preparation of this handbook it became clear that a composite Service Book, also sponsored by all the participating Churches, would be welcomed and found pastorally helpful in crematoria and cemetery chapels.

The efforts of the Churches' Funerals Group have made it possible to produce this service book, containing as it does within one volume a set of funeral services which includes at least one service that can be used by each of the Communions represented on the Churches' Funerals Group according to the circumstances of the occasion. (A companion edition has in the past been produced in consultation with the Free Church Council of Wales containing versions of two services and eight hymns in the Welsh language.)

Funeral Service prepared by the Joint Liturgical Group

The Joint Liturgical Group was formed in 1963 and is a Formal Network of Churches Together in Britain and Ireland. It includes representatives of the Church of England, the Church of Scotland, the Scottish Episcopal Church, the Church in Wales, the Greek Orthodox Archdiocese of

127

Thyateira and Great Britain, the Baptist Union of Great Britain, the Roman Catholic, Methodist and United Reformed Churches, the Connexion of independent Methodist Churches, the Congregational Federation and Churches Together in Britain and Ireland. The Joint Liturgical Group provides liturgical texts and other resources, deals with questions relating to public worship of ecumenical concern and organises conferences on such matters.

Church of England Services

Roman Catholic Services

Selection of Hymns

The following hymns are copyright and used with permission:

Page	First line
90	*Great is thy faithfulness, O God my Father*

William Runyan (1870–1957)/Thomas O Chisholm (1866–1960). © 1923 Renewed 1951 Hope Publishing, administered by CopyCare, PO Box 77, Hailsham, East Sussex BN27 3EF (music@copycare.com). Used by permission.

93   *I am the Bread of Life*
S. Suzanne Toolan (b. 1927). © 1966 by GIA Publications Inc. 7404 S.Mason Avenue, Chicago, Illinois 60638. All rights reserved. Used with permission.

101   *Lord of all hopefulness, Lord of all joy*
Words by Jan Struther (1901–1953) from 'Enlarged Songs of Praise'. © By Permission of Oxford Union Press, Great Clarendon Street, Oxford OX2 6DP.

104   *Make me a channel of your peace*
Sebastian Temple (1928–1997). © OCP Publications, 5536 N.E.Hassalo, Portland, OR 97213, USA. All rights reserved. Used with permission.

105   *Morning has broken, like the first morning*
Eleanor Farjeon (1881–1965) From 'The Childrens Bells' (OUP). © David Higham Associates Ltd, 5–8 Lower John Street, Golden Square, London W1F 9HA. Used by permission.

110   *O Lord my God, when I in awesome wonder*
© 1953 Stuart K Hine/the Stuart Hine Trust. Published by Kingsway's Thankyou Music, PO Box 75, Eastbourne, East Sussex BN23 6NW. Worldwide (excluding North and South America). Used by permission.

112   *On a hill far away stood an old rugged cross*
George Bennard (1873–1958). © Word Music Inc, administered by CopyCare, PO Box 77, Hailsham, East Sussex BN27 3EF (music@copycare.com). Used by permission.

121   *There is a Redeemer*
Melody Green. © 1984 Ears to Hear Music/Birdwing Music/BMG Songs Inc/ EMI Christian Music Publishing, administered by CopyCare, PO Box 77, Hailsham, East Sussex BN27 3EF (music@copycare.com). Used by permission.

122   *Thine be the glory, risen, conquering Son*
Tr. Edmond Budry (1854–1932) and Richard Hoyle (1875–1939). © By permission of the World Student Christian Federation, 5 Route des Morillons, 1218 Grand-Saconnex, Geneva, Switzerland.